MEDIATION OF DECONSTRUCTION

BERNARD LONERGAN'S METHOD IN PHILOSOPHY

The Argument from Human Operational Development

Martin Joseph Matustik

UNIVERSITY
PRESS OF
AMERICA

Lanham • New York • London

University Press of America,® Inc.

4720 Boston Way
Lanham, MD 20706

3 Henrietta Street
London WC2E 8LU England

Printed in the United States of America

British Cataloging in Publication Information Available

ISBN: 0-8191-6762-2 (pbk. : alk. paper)
ISBN: 0-8191-6761-4 (alk. paper)

All University Press of America books are produced on acid-free paper which exceeds the minimum standards set by the National Historical Publications and Records Commission.

TABLE OF CONTENTS

EPILOGUE

LIST OF TABLES

PREFACE

This is an interpretation of Bernard Lonergan's use of the notion of mediation in his thematization of human operational development.[1] In discovering Lonergan, I discovered not so much the content of the answers sought for, but the exigencies of my questioning. These exigencies were operative implicitly in various experiences: of making sense of the Communist régime in Czechoslovakia; of the "Prague Spring" and its supression by the Soviet invasion in 1968; of the Socratic death of the Czech philosopher and a student of E. Husserl, professor Jan Patočka, who also became the spokesman for the human rights dissent in Czechoslovakia called CHARTA 77; of my almost a year-long stay in an Austrian refugee camp; of the inverted world of Western brands of oppression and unfreedom; and of the paradox-and-tragedy embedded in the human condition under which I in the United States and my family and friends in Central Europe contribute indirectly work and directly taxes to our mutual nuclear annihilation.

What stands over and against a mutual annihilation is mutual self-mediation, i.e., programmatic organon for an ongoing collaboration within the pluralistic contexts of variously differentiated consciousness of the individuals and cultures. Lonergan proposes in "The Mediation of Christ in Prayer, " and in his other major works, a form of an argument that relies not so much on principles of logic, as on one's methodical explicitation of hope operative implicitly in mutual, self-mediating de-

---

[1]Cf. the previously unpublished lecture by Lonergan, "The Mediation of Christ in Prayer" [1963], edited by Mark D. Morelli in <u>Method: Journal of Lonergan Studies</u>, Vol. 2, No. 1 (March, 1984), and also M. D. Morelli's editorial comment preceding this lecture in the same issue of <u>Method</u> for the inspiration of this study.

velopment towards authentic freedom. Insofar as Lonergan's argument aims at clearing up the weeds of common bias, it is a form of ideology critique; inasmuch as Lonergan enters various human discourses in order to reveal the roots of bias, his project engenders a type of 'deconstruction' of these discourses; but because Lonergan's program is primarily an invitation to one's self-apppropriation of his or her operational development, there is no such a thing as a single, or clear and distinct, "Lonerganian Argument."

What precedes Lonergan's full use of mediation, is his 'deconstruction' of different discourses into which he entered: Aquinas, history of mathematical and natural sciences, religion, art, the German historical school, philosophy, and economics.[2] In my argument that Lonergan's project is a type of 'deconstruction' of the various discourses into which he entered, I have drawn upon the works by Jacques Derrida and other standard commentaries on deconstruction.[3] My purpose in using Derrida will be to distinguish his sense of deconstruction from that of Lonergan; discussion of Derrida's notion of deconstruction will dominate in Chapter I, Lonergan's in the rest of the study. My citation of Michel Foucault[4] is by way of an example. Lonergan was familiar with M. Foucault's work.[5] This secondary

----

[2]By 'deconstruction', I mean taking apart what has been constructed, in order to retrieve a point of assembly. What is the meaning of this point will vary among different thinkers of post-structuralist thought and, more importantly, from the sense implied in Lonergan's methodology.

[3]My most extensive references to Derrida will be in Chapter I, section D., subsection 2., on "Structuralism, deconstruction, and Lonergan's notion of mediation as a dynamic structure."

[4]Chapter IV, section D.

[5]The reader should note Lonergan's references to L. Binswanger's work with a 130 pages long Preface by M. Foucault, first mentioned by B. Lonergan in his unpublished <u>Philosophy of Education</u>, 1959.

literature is in support of my main project which is the interpretation of Lonergan's notion of mediation. One's understanding of mediation is, also, crucial for contemporary dialogue with thinkers like Kojève, Derrida, Foucault, and Rorty.[6]

Since Lonergan's notion of mediation was not extensively treated as a topic in published scholarly studies, I will draw primarily on Lonergan's own published and unpublished thematization of the problem of mediation. I refer to other philosophers but (with the exception of Derrida and Foucault) only inasmuch as Lonergan brings them into his treatment of the development of meaning, and I limit myself to Lonergan's interpretation of the history of philosophy without trying to do any comparative work, e.g., on Hegel's or Marxist use of mediation and Lonergan's transposition of Hegel's or Marxist use. To my knowledge, no one has yet undertaken to interpret the notion of mediation as a specific point from which to understand Lonergan's project. David Tracy, for example, prefers 'horizon-analysis' to 'mediation' in his <u>The Achievement of Bernard Lonergan</u>, although he does extensively interpret Lonergan's thematization of meaning and the self-constitutive function of consciousness.[7]

Lonergan's account of consciousness as self-constituting is crucial to an adequate understanding of his argument from self-mediation by human operational development. In the manuscript <u>On the Ontological and Psychological Constitution of Christ</u> (1956-58), and then in his reply to objections in "Christ as Subject: A Reply" (1959), where he first

---

[6]See the Bibliography.

[7]<u>The Achievement of Bernard Lonergan</u> (1970) was his published doctoral thesis. Here, while he uses the then unpublished materials for Lonergan's later <u>Method in Theology</u> (1972), he defers the notion of 'mediation' to future research and takes the term 'horizon-analysis' as his primary focus when interpreting the stages of development of Lonergan's thought.

treated of consciousness in depth, Lonergan distinguishes between the views that take consciousness to be another perception or operation and his own, that specifies consciousness as experience. In his lectures on Existentialism given at Boston College (1957), he brings his analysis of consciousness to bear on his argument for the psychological presence of the subject as subject. I use his formulation of the argument, as found in the above lectures, to underline the negative aspect of the denial of psychological self-presence. If the self-constitutive function of consciousness is eclipsed either by faulty introspection or by other theories of subjectivity, there result the death of the subject and the end of history. This is what Lonergan probably has in mind when he speaks of the contemporary neglected subject.

In his interpretation of Jean Piaget's findings,[8] Lonergan highlights the distinction between the structures of perception and those of basic operations. The point of the distinction is parallel to his analysis of consciousness: primacy belongs to the operational development, adaptation, grouping, and mediation. Against N. Chomsky and the structuralist concern with the unconscious, deep structures, Lonergan argues that development is made possible because of the intentional, self-transcending dynamism of consciousness.

Lonergan's early use of mediation appears in his Latin notes De methodo theologiae (1962), in the summer institute held in Toronto, "Method of Theology" (1962), in his Montreal lectures "Time and Meaning" (1962) and "The Mediation of Christ in Prayer" (1963), and in the subsequent thematizations of the development of meaning (the last two papers published in Collection, the whole of A Second Collection, A Third Collection, and Method in Theology). I compare Lonergan's use of David Hilbert's concept

---

[8]Lonergan's references to Piaget's research first appear in the manuscript on Philosophy of Education, 1959.

of implicit definition in Insight with a fully developed notion of mediation, and Lonergan's general account of development in the chapter on "Genetic Method," in Insight, with his more specific treatment of development of meaning in terms of operational analysis. In "Time and Meaning," Lonergan stresses that Piaget's description of the stages in the child development inspired him to come up with a theoretical structure of development in general and broaden his account of genetic method.

In his 1962 institute on "Method of Theology," Lonergan introduces the topic of the three fundamental antitheses, or "blocks," in human development: the sacred-profane, common sense-theory, and exteriority-interiority. The blocks represent the stages both in the ontogeny of the individual and in history of culture(s). As in child development so in cultural history, one can distinguish the stages of operations on meaning and value and, similarly, the differentiations of consciousness. With the developed notions of meaning and mediation, Lonergan is able to sharpen his account of the self-constitutive character of consciousness and distinguish the worlds of immediacy, those mediated and constituted by meaning, and the exigencies (controls) of meaning and value. Now the implicit definition (in Hilbert's sense) of culture is possible in terms of undifferentiated and differentiated consciousness and its mediating and controlling functions. Finally, the three fundamental antitheses form the mediating phase of method considering the past, and the past is mediated through a methodical exigence of meaning that regards the future (mediated phase).

Critical and methodical mediation of meaning and value results in an upheaval of the subject: Intellectual, moral, and religious conversions effect a 'decentering' or 'deconstruction' upwards of the human subject, i.e., by reorganization of one's operational development.[9] Lonergan's life-long enter-

----

[9]The terms 'deconstruction' and 'decentering' are not Lonergan's; nevertheless, I find them fitting in light of a needed dialogue with other the projects

prise and his entry into many fields of human discourses can be thematized in terms of 'deconstruction' of science, history, Thomism, theology, philosophy, and economics. His 'deconstruction' of historical consciousness is not a displacement downwards, to the points of assembly with minimal intelligibility, but rather upwards, i.e., through one's self-appropriation of operational development for the sake of heightening functions of affect and intelligence.

I have opted for a more radical reading of Lonergan over and against the tamed Lonergan. The latter is mostly in a dialogue with the Catholic, Scholastic, and Thomistic tradition, or stays within the immediate circle of Lonerganians; the former has much to mediate and communicate in the secular world by way of programmatic 'deconstruction' of the roots of contemporary post-modern, totalitarian, or nihilistic one-dimensional thinking and living, together with 'deconstruction' of their themes: the death of 'god', the death of the human subject, and the end of history.[10]

Lonergan's method in philosophy is, thus, neither a form of new scholasticism, nor a post-modern fury of suspicion; rather, his method of 'deconstruction' is foundational in its self-appropriating recovery of attentive, intelligent, reasonable, and responsible subject in an argument from human operational development. The fact that

----

of "archeology" and "genealogy" of human subjectivity.

[10]This reading places Lonergan in the midst of contemporary discussions among the "masters of suspicion" (Foucault, Lacan, Derrida, Deleuze, Rorty), "masters of recovery" (Habermas, Ricoeur, Metz), and those who are searching for a rapprochement among the diverse traditions of the Anglo-American analytic thought, philosophy of science, Pragmatism, and Continental philosophy (e.g. Rorty, Bernstein, Dallmayr, Lamb).

both the tamed and the radical streams of interpretation are possible, perhaps, points out the way in which the method in philosophy undertaken by Lonergan incorporates, sublates, and opens a novel, mediated phase of human development.

Due to cultural confusion about the use of the generic noun 'man' and the related pronouns such as 'he', 'his', 'him', or 'himself' when referring to the human subject, the scientist, or the philosopher, and in order to avoid sexism in language; the word 'man' will denote only a particular male individual, and the pronouns such as 'he', 'his', 'him', or 'himself' will be alternated by paragraphs with the feminine pronouns 'she', 'hers', 'her', 'herself' when referring to the human subject, the scientist, the philosopher, or similar cases. No alterations will be made in the cited passages, unless the contexts requires it. The single quotation marks will enclose philosophical and theological terms set off for emphasis, with the exception of J. Derrida's term deconstruction that will be enclosed in single quotation marks only when referring specifically to a 'deconstruction' implied in Lonergan's methodology. Lonergan's main technical expressions will be underlined when they appear in the exposition for the first time, and then whenever the context calls for it.

There are many whom I would like to thank for inspiration and encouragement during the time of my research and writing this study. There is Dr. James L. Marsh, Dr. Richard J. Blackwell, and Dr. Vincent Ch. Punzo at St. Louis University; Fr. Robert Doran, S.J., Dr. Patrick Byrne, Fr. Joseph Flanagan, S.J., Dr. Fred Lawrence, Fr. Frederick Crowe, S.J., Dr. Mark Morelli, Fr. Timothy Fallon, S.J. involved in Lonergan studies in various parts of the academic community; Fr. James Bernauer, S.J., Fr. William Richardson, S.J. at Boston College; and my friend James Duffy. All of these made some critical input at different stages of the development of the ideas in this study and for that, and their friendship and encouragement, I am most grateful.

ABBREVIATIONS

(Works by Lonergan cited and abbreviated in the notes)

AM "The Analogy of Meaning"
BTI "Belief: Today's Issue"
CAM *Caring about Meaning*
Coll. *Collection*
CRIS "Critical Realism and the Integration of the Sciences"
CS "Cognitional Structure"
CSR "Christ as Subject: A Reply"
DM "Dimensions of Meaning"
DMT *De methodo theologiae*
DD "The Dehellenization of Dogma"
DP *Doctrinal Pluralism*
EA "*Existenz* and *Aggiornamento*"
ECA *An Essay in Circulation Analysis*
FT "The Future of Thomism"
GMC "The Absence of God in Modern Culture"
HCH "Healing and Creating in History"
IBL "An Interview with Fr. Bernard Lonergan, S.J."
Insight *Insight: A Study of Human Understanding*
LML "Lectures on Mathematical Logic"
M "Mediation"
MCI "Meaning as a Category for Interpretation"
MCP "The Mediation of Christ in Prayer"
MH "Merging Horizons: System, Common Sense, Scholarship"
MIT *Method in Theology*
MoT "Method of Theology"
NE "Notes on Existentialism"
OPC *On the Ontological and Psychological Constitution of Christ*
OPI "The Original Preface of *Insight*"
PE *Philosophy of Education*
PGT *Philosophy of God, and Theology*
QP "Questionnaire on Philosophy"
RE "Religious Experience"
SC *A Second Collection*
Sub. "The Subject"
TC *A Third Collection*
TDE "(Towards) a Definition of Education"
TM "Time and Meaning"
UB *Understanding and Being*
VWIA *Verbum: Word and Idea in Aquinas*
WCLS "What is Claude Lévi-Strauss up to?"

PART ONE:

THE NOTION OF MEDIATION

If you want to find out anything from the theoretical physicists about the methods they use, I advise you to stick closely to one principle: don't listen to their words, fix your attention on their deeds.

Albert Einstein, *Essays in Science* (New York: Philosophical Library, 1934), p. 12.

CHAPTER I

MEDIATION AS A DYNAMIC STRUCTURE OF FUNCTIONAL RELATIONSHIPS

An Introduction

Bernard Lonergan introduces the notion of mediation as a means of classifying the functional relationships (1) between basic and derived terms and (2) in development, between the basic group of operations and higher, differentiated stages of mediate operations. Accordingly, Lonergan's methodological analysis is immediately of operations but mediately through the operations. It is immediately of operations insofar as it considers the group of operations by which the object of investigation is reached. It is mediately through the operations, for while Lonergan's analysis begins from data, it is principally concerned with the operational development of the human subject.[1]

----

[1]Bernard Lonergan, "Method of Theology," lectures (Toronto: Regis College, 1962); unpublished transcription of the summer institute from the tapes by John Brezovec (Toronto: Regis College, Lonergan Institute, 1980), pp. 1-3; cf. p. 107. [Hereafter abbreviated as MoT with references to the manuscript by Brezovec.]

The structure of Lonergan's summer institute on Method follows the Latin course taught by Lonergan at the Gregorian University, Rome, in 1961-62 and 1963-64, which is preserved in the Latin notes taken by the graduate students in Rome under the title De methodo theologiae, notae desumptae ab alumnis (Rome: Gregorian University, 1962). [Hereafter abbreviated as DMT.]

The first fourteen lectures of the Toronto Institute contain two chapters from the Latin course taught in Rome and six additional lectures. The transcript by Brezovec is thus divided into ch. 1 on method in general and ch. 2, which has two sections: (1) on theology as science and three fundamental antitheses, (2) the theological problems based on

LONERGAN'S MEDIATION OF DECONSTRUCTION

In this chapter, I will give an exposition of the set of basic terms and analogies that Lonergan derives from the notion of mediation. In my exposition, I will draw upon his previously unpublished 1963 Gonzaga University lecture "The Mediation of Christ in Prayer."[2] First, I will introduce Lonergan's notion of mediation in three sections: A. Mediation in General, B. Mutual Mediation, and C. Self-Mediation: Living.

Secondly, in section D., I will discuss my exposition of Lonergan's treatment of mediation: (1) a dynamic structure of mediation (this will include an account of his meaning of 'structure'), (2) the relationship of Lonergan's notion of mediation as a dynamic structure to the tenets of structuralism and deconstruction, and (3) I will conclude with a brief account of the classical, statistical, genetic, and dialectical methods of investigation described and related to mediation by Lonergan.

The three subsequent chapters of Part Two will then take up Lonergan's methodological analysis proper, namely, self-mediation in human operational development: (II) Consciousness as Self-Constituting, (III) Consciousness as Mediated by

----

these three antitheses. The sections added by Lonergan in Toronto comprise lecture 15 on positive and systematic theology; lecture 16 on meaning; lectures 17 and 18 on hermeneutics; and lectures 19 and 20 on history.

On the notion of _mediation_, see MoT, pp. 96-99 and 106-109; on _basis_ and _expansion_ in the method of metaphysics, see Bernard Lonergan, _Insight: A Study of Human Understanding_ (New York: Philosophical Library, and London: Longmans, Green and Company, 1957), pp. 386-87. [Hereafter abbreviated as _Insight_.] Consult Fig. 1 _infra_.

[2]Bernard Lonergan, "The Mediation of Christ in Prayer," _Method: Journal Of Lonergan Studies_ Vol. 2, No. 1 (March 1984): 1-20. [Hereafter abbreviated as MCP.] The lecture was originally given at Thomas More Institute in Montreal, on September 24, 1963. See also editor's summary preceeding the paper in the above issue of _Method_.

Meaning, and (IV) Consciousness as Differentiated Through Controls of Meaning and Value. In concluding section of the fourth chapter, I will consolidate Lonergan's argument from human development by focusing on the three aspects that converge in his notion of mediation: first, the prior development mediates a later development; secondly, a development in one field affects the other fields; thirdly, all development mediates the subject as self-constitutive and self-transcending source of possible further development.[3]

A. Mediation in General

Lonergan begins his account of mediation with a brief consideration of Aristotle's and Hegel's use of the notion of mediation. Aristotle employed mediation within the field of classical logic. He distinguished *immediate* first principles, *mediate* middle term shared by the subject and the predicate, and *mediated* conclusion; further, in the *Posterior Analytics* he established relations between these three terms on the basis of the syllogism.[4] The first principles are said to be immediately self-evident because they cannot be proved nor do they admit of a middle term (a logical proof "proves" only insofar as a middle term links the subject and the attribute). The middle term mediates between subject and predicate; and the concluded predicate is thus mediated in the subject.

Hegel's idealist philosophy, according to Lonergan, extended the notion of mediation to everything by endowing it with a universal role: (1) concepts can be related either immediately or mediately, (2) but all reduces to concepts, (3) so everything is related immediately or mediately. It must follow that the relations between concepts as found on any inferior level prior to their attainment to the fullness of the universal concept (the *Begriff*) are imperfect.[5]

----

[3]MoT, pp. 106-109.

[4]References by Lonergan are made to Aristotle's *Posterior Analytics*, Bk. II, 4; cf. see MCP, p. 20, n. 2; also MoT, p. 99.

In his lecture, "The Mediation of Christ in Prayer," Lonergan proposes a transposition of both the Aristotelian and Hegelian notions of mediation in the following way: With respect to Hegel, he wants to use the word 'mediation' in a universal manner but without any implications of idealism;[6] with respect to Aristotle, he wants to generalize the relations of the terms in Aristotelian logic by leaving out the classicist assumptions of self-evident necessity and truth as simply given in immediate first principles and their mediated conclusions.[7]

By these generalizations, Lonergan introduces the axiom of general patterns of structures: "any factor, quality, property, feature, aspect" is (1) mediate and may be considered to be (2) immediate in "the source, origin, ground, basis" and (3) mediated in "its consequences, effects, derivations, outcome, field of influence, radiation, expansion, expression, manifestation, revelation."[8]

----

[5]MCP, pp. 1-2. References by Lonergan are made to Hegel's Phänomenologie, and Gaston Fessard's De l'actualité historique, Vol. I (Paris: Desclée de Brouwer, 1960); and on the notion of mediation in Hegel to Henri Niel's De la Médiation dans la Philosophie de Hegel (Paris: Aubier, 1945). On Hegel see also Bernard Lonergan, Understanding And Being: A Companion to Insight, the Halifax Lectures by Bernard Lonergan, edited by Elizabeth and Mark Morelli (New York: The Edwin Mellen Press, 1980), pp. 310-11. [Hereafter abbreviated as UB.]

See also comments in MoT, p. 96, on Hegel's notion of 'sublation' of religion by philosophy and of art by religion, and p. 100 on Hegel's early studies of interiority and his later fully developed dialectic. Consult Insight on sublation and Aufhebung, pp. 374 and 422; on Hegelian dialectic, pp. 372-74, 422-23, 594; and on difference of Lonergan's notion of dialectic from that of Hegel, p. 564.

[6]MCP, p. 2.

[7]Ibid.

[8]Ibid.

MEDIATION AS A DYNAMIC STRUCTURE

The result of this transposed notion of mediation takes a form which is "more general than the notion of causality," for it does not settle anything "specific, or even anything determinately generic."[9] The advantage Lonergan finds in its generality is not the vagueness of the notion, but the patterning "that the notion of mediation itself can accept."[10] In its most general expression, mediation is defined functionally by a base in the source and the categorial realizations that derive from the dynamism of the source (hence, the basic and derived terms). The more complex instances of this general axiom are either variables of the initial pattern (mutual mediation) or the higher differentiations of development (self-mediation).

Next, Lonergan illustrates the general theorem of mediation by four examples taken from mechanics, from organic and psychic life, and from logic. First, a watch is a mechanical example of mediation in general. The watch is said to be immediate in the movement of the mainspring and mediated in the movement of the other parts. Further, the function of a watch is the control of timed movement. This function of control is immediate in the source (the balance wheel) and mediated in the outcome (the movement of the subsequent series of wheels and levers).[11]

Secondly, there is an organic example of various mediate functions: the supply of oxygen, the flow of blood, nutrition, locomotion and the nervous control of the organism. The supply of oxygen is immediate in the respiratory system and mediated in the body; the flow of blood is immediate in the pumping of the heart and mediated in the rest of the body; nutrition is immediate in digestive system and mediated in the whole body; locomotion is immediate in the skeleto-muscular system and mediated in the movement of the whole body; and, finally, nervous control is immediate in the nervous system and mediated in the whole body.[12]

----

[9]Ibid.
[10]Ibid.
[11]Ibid., p. 3.
[12]Ibid.

Thirdly, in psychic life, what is immediate in intelligence, or will, imagination, affects, memory, etc., is mediated in the rest of consciousness and in the bodily expressions.[13] For example, one's anger is immediate in aggressivity and mediated in the expressions of the eyes, the tone of one's voice, in one's violent images or one's raised arms.

Fourthly, a logical example of mediation in general is the Aristotelian syllogism. Truth, evidence, and necessity are immediate in the first principles "not because something else but because of the nature of first principles themselves."[14] Truth, evidence, and necessity are mediated in conclusions.

B. Mutual Mediation

The notion of mediation becomes more interesting with further complications. Mutual mediation is a case of the functional whole, namely, the whole as "constituted by mutually mediating parts."[15] Lonergan gives again four illustrations.

First, a watch may be considered as a material whole or a functional whole. The former refers to what "is the case and what is in the case."[16] The latter considers a watch according to what it does, i.e., keep time. Keeping time will depend on the movement in the watch and on the constant rate of that movement. The function of the movement (f1) is immediate in the mainspring and mediated in the rest of the wheels and levers. The function of steady movement (f2) is immediate in the balance wheel and mediated in the rest of the wheels and levers. The functional whole is constituted by the mutual mediation of f1 (movement of the mainspring) and f2 (control in the balance wheel). Thus, f1 moves itself and the balance wheel, f2 controls itself and the mainspring. Mutual mediation of f1 (movement) and f2

----

[13]Ibid.
[14]Ibid., p. 4.
[15]Ibid.
[16]Ibid.

(control) is immediate in the respective functions (f1, f2) and mediated in their mutual mediation (keeping time).[17]

Secondly, an organism may be considered either as a material whole, e.g., "the skin and what is inside it," or as a functional whole.[18] In case of mutual mediation, a functional whole, one may prescind from taking into account the organism as living.[19] The organism, as functional whole, is immediately supplied by oxygen in the respiratory system, by nutrition in the digestive tract, controlled in the nervous system, supplied by locomotion in the muscles, and mediately supplied in the rest of the whole body. The immediate function f1 (A,B,C, D...) and the mediated functions f2 (a,b,c,d...) are mutually mediated as a functional whole {f1(A)f2 (a,b,c,d...)}, {f1(B)f2 (a,b,c,d...)}, {f1(C)f2 (a,b,c,d...)}, etc.[20]

Thirdly, anger was said to be immediate in aggressivity and mediated in the look of one's eyes, in the tone of one's voice, violent images and memories, vigor of the will, etc.[21] But anger is also a case of mutual mediation:

> [B]ecause what one sees, feels, remembers, imagines, thinks, wills, feeds one's anger. The anger grows and one tends toards an explosion. There is a muual mediation or a feedback from the results of anger to its causes.[22]

Fourthly, Aristotelian logic accepts only one immediate center (necessity, evidence, truth in the

----

[17]Ibid.

[18]Ibid.

[19]Ibid., p. 5. I will return to a consideration of the organism as living when treating the notion of self-mediation.

[20]Cf. Ibid.

[21]Ibid.

[22]Ibid.

first principles) and all else is mediated.[23] A logical example of a mutual mediation is an empirical science where there are discernible two immediates. An empirical science is a functional whole: (f1) it is empirical immediately "through its attention to data," and mediated in empirical science; (f2) it is scientific immediately in "intellectual effort and work, in the inquiries, insights, hypotheses, and deductions," and mediated in empirical science.[24] A mutual mediation of the two centers of immediacy, the lower blade comprising attention to empirical data and the upper blade of the recurrent operations of the scientific inquiry, creates the functional whole (what Lonergan elsewhere calls a scissors-like movement of two blades) of an empirical science.[25]

Final note: As in the previous example of the organic functional whole, Lonergan prescinded from treating the organism *qua* alive, so also his examples of psychic and logical mutual mediation speak about conscious operations without the benefit of the reader knowing what Lonergan means by consciousness. Both life and consciousness must be considered as more complicated stages or extensions of an applied pattern of mediation.

C. Self-Mediation: Living

Lonergan introduces the general definition of self-mediation: "a whole that has consequences that change the whole."[26] While machines, electronic computers, and organisms all are functional wholes, only organisms exhibit self-mediation through operational development. First, there is the self- origination in an organism of growth by its physical parts. This self-origination proceeds through a process of division to 2*n* cells.[27] Growth and division are marked

---

[23]Ibid.

[24]Ibid.

[25]Ibid., p. 6. I will return to Lonergan's metaphor of "scissors-like" movement of inquiry in ch. IV.

[26]Ibid.

[27]Ibid.

by a finality, for they are not governed by geometric patterns but by "a certain finality within the organism itself."[28] Both machines and organisms are functional wholes; but whereas the former are made, the latter grow.

There are stages in the life of an organism. In any particular stage, the organism is a functional whole with different centers of immediacy mediated in the functioning of the whole body. But there emerge patterns that regard functions both now and in the future. These are the transitional and anticipatory developments in living.[29] An example of the former is the infant feeding at the breast: infant's ability is useful for a time but will later disappear. The latter is exemplified by the size of the infant's brain which is not functionally useful to the rest of the child's body: the size of the brain has no great function during infancy but will be essential later on.[30]

Secondly, the anticipatory developments lead to processes of specialization and differentiation that are more than a case of mutual mediation. "The process of specialization involves the creation and exploitation of entirely new possibilities."[31] Self-mediation in the development of the organisms changes the whole by displacement upwards:

> In this self-mediation of the first kind--the development of the organism--there is a displacement upwards, a displacement from the one or 2*n* cells to the life of the organism, which is something different from the life of the cells. The *telos* is the self-developing and self-sustaining functional whole that develops through the development and

----

[28]Ibid. Lonergan refers here to Van Driesch's experiments on sea urchins.
[29]Ibid.
[30]Ibid.
[31]Ibid., p. 7.

> functions through functioning of its parts.[32]

Finally, besides growth of the corresponding functions, differentiation and specialization, and a single development of any particular living organism, there is "the larger whole of the concrete universal."[33] The notion of mediation is applicable not only to interrelations between the individual and species, within the species as such, but also to the interrelations among different species. Lonergan thematizes reproduction and species development functionally, in non-Darwinian, emergent terms: (1) the species mediates itself by the reproduction of the individuals; (2) "within the genus, lower species mediate the emergence and the sustenance of higher species";[34] and (3) ecologically speaking, lower life mediates the emergence and the sustenance of higher life in the self-mediation of the living environment.[35] A succinct summary of the corresponding and emergent functions in self-mediation through living is offered in Insight, in the chapter on "The Notion of Development":

> [A] development may be defined as a flexible, linked sequence of dynamic and increasingly differeniated higher integrations that meet the tension of successively trans-

----

[32]Ibid.

[33]Ibid. (italics mine).

[34]Ibid. On Lonergan's reference to Darwin see the interviews with B. Lonergan in Pierrot Cambert, Charlotte Tansey, Cathleen Going, eds. Caring about Meaning: Patterns in the life of Bernard Lonergan (Montreal, Quebec: Thomas More Institute, 1982), pp. 212ff.: Lonergan--". . . Darwin can be used in emergent probability. Probabilities of emergence and probabilities of survival are the two sets of probabilities with regard to anything. . . . It was my transposition of Darwin. . . . Darwin has 'survival of the fittest,' and chance variations. For me, chance is occurrence of the improbable." [Hereafter abbreviated as CAM.]

[35]MCP, pp. 7-8.

> formed underlying manifolds through successive applications of the principle of correspondence and emergence.[36]

D. Discussion

In my foregoing exposition of Lonergan's lecture "The Mediation of Christ in Prayer," the notion of mediation was considered from its material and formal aspects. The former is expressed in the universal theorem that distinguishes between a source and whatever results from it. The latter yields to a more complex patterning: mediation in general, mutual mediation, and self-mediation. The methodological analysis of mediation described by Lonergan thus (1) proceeds from a dynamic structure of functional relationships between the basic and derived terms, and (2) expands through development of the basic and differentiated groups of operations.

In this section, I will (1) discuss what Lonergan means by a dynamic structure of mediation, (2) clarify the relationship of his meaning of 'a dynamic structure' to the tenets of structuralism and deconstruction, and (3) describe Lonergan's account of the classical, statistical, genetic, and dialectical methods of investigation pertaining to the basic and differentiated dynamic structure of mediation.

In my discussion, I will draw upon Lonergan's Dublin lectures on _Insight_ (1961),[37] and his paper "Cognitional Structure,"[38] where he states what he

----

[36]_Insight_, p. 454. On the principle of emergence and correspondence, and on finality see _Insight_, pp. 451ff.

[37]Bernard Lonergan, "Critical Realism and the Integration of the Sciences," (Dublin: University College, May 23-25, 1961); six lectures on _Insight_ and an appendix with question and answer period; unpublished manuscript available at the Lonergan Institute, Regis College, Toronto. [Hereafter abbreviated as CRIS.]

[38]Bernard Lonergan, "Cognitional Structure," in

means by a dynamic structure. The examples used in the lectures, and the summary of the structural relationship between a whole and its parts offered in the paper, parallel both my foregoing exposition of Lonergan's notion of mediation in "The Mediation of Christ in Prayer" (1963)[39] and his 1978 lecture "What is Claude Lévi-Strauss Up To?" given at the Toronto conference on hermeneutics and structuralism.[40]

My purpose in bringing these four apparently disparate works by Lonergan together and drawing upon them in this section is two-fold: In the first place, I wish to trace Lonergan's development and broad use of the notion of mediation, and to link this notion with his earlier treatment of implicit definition in Insight. In the second place, in my clarification of the relationship between Lonergan's account of a dynamic structure and the tenets of structuralism and deconstruction, I will suggest that his use of mediation engenders a project of 'deconstruction' of the various discourses into which he entered. To substantiate my assertion of Lonergan's 'deconstruction' and to differentiate it from Derrida and other post-structuralist projects of deconstruc-

----

Collection: Papers by Bernard Lonergan, S.J. Edited and introd. by Fred E. Crowe, S.J. (London: Darton, Longman & Todd, and New York: Herder & Herder, 1967). [Hereafter "Cognitional Structure" abbreviated as CS with references to Collection, abbreviated as Coll.]

[39]In an outline for the Gonzaga lecture on "Mediation" (Spokane: Gonzaga University, 1963; unpublished draft available at the Lonergan Institute, Regis College, Toronto), Lonergan states his purpose [p. 1]: "To reach a positive account of whole and part, and so to move towards a positive statement of Newman's theorem. To introduce a number of basic terms and analogies in a coherent and systematic fashion."

[Hereafter abbreviated as M.]

[40]Bernard Lonergan, "What is Claude Lévi-Strauss Up To?" (Toronto: Regis College, 1978); unpublished lecture is available at the Lonergan Institute, Regis College, Toronto.

[Hereafter abbreviated as WCLS.]

tion will be one of the tasks of the argument I develop throughout the subsequent chapters in Part Two of this study.

(1) A dynamic structure of mediation

First, I will give an account of what Lonergan means by a dynamic structure and, secondly, show how this account relates both to mediation and his treatment of definition in Insight.

While the notion of structure appears to be "a very modern word," says Lonergan, "it is the old idea of the whole and the part."[41] What is said about a source and an outcome may be expressed in structural terms. A whole of mediation consists of parts and thus forms a structure: "The whole is related to each of the parts, and each of the parts is related to the other parts and to the whole."[42] Parts may be considered as either materially or functionally related, and a whole of mediation as either materially or formally dynamic.

Material parts are arrived at by division, e.g., by slicing a piece of pie or drawing a semi-circle. Now a pie also consists of functional parts, such as the crust and the filling, namely, the functions of containing and being contained.[43] Functional parts can be expressed in a proportion: "crust is to filling as container to contained."[44] Analogically, a materially dynamic whole may consist of material parts, e.g., components in the architectural structure, or of activities, as in singing, dancing, performing a symphony or acting in a drama.[45] On the other hand, a formally dynamic structure is not restricted to the parts, but exhibits an additional ability to assemble and constitute itself as a whole of mutual and self- mediation.

To illustrate: The clock can be taken apart and

----

[41]CRIS, p. 14.
[42]CS, in Coll. p. 222.
[43]CRIS, p. 14.
[44]Ibid.
[45]CS, in Coll. p. 222.

put together according to a diagram without understanding anything about the function of measuring time.[46] One deals simply with material parts, such as the wheels and the rest of the works. To grasp the function of a timepiece is to understand a source of its power in the mainspring, the relations of series of levers to the function of a pendulum and an escapement.[47] The functional parts are partial and complementary: one "cannot predicate the part of the whole or the whole of the part."[48] Neither the pendulum, nor the mainspring, nor the levers are enough in themselves, but rather as functional parts they comprise "an internal and complete set of partial and complementary functions."[49] The above illustration defines Lonergan's meaning of 'structure':

> Abstractly structure denotes the internally closed set of relations between parts; concretely the structure is the complete set of parts as informed by those relations, and consequently, the structure is the same thing as the whole *qua* whole, the whole plus the reason why it is a whole.[50]

Given this account of structure, "one can go on to distinguish isomorphic and analogous structures and dynamic and static structures and so on."[51] Lonergan's introduction of the notion of mediation in its material and formal aspects serves him in this very task as a methodological tool for classifying basic, derived, and higher differentiations of structural relationships.

The import of Lonergan's fully thematized notion of mediation is twofold: (1) the notion unifies the matter of the first five chapters of *Insight* and the section on *genetic method* in chapter XV of the same

----

[46]CRIS, p. 14.
[47]Ibid., p. 15.
[48]Ibid.
[49]Ibid.
[50]Ibid.
[51]Ibid., p. 16.

work under a single methodological consideration, and (2) besides the analysis of the objects in their functional relations and of development in self-mediating operations of life, the notion pertains directly to Lonergan's later explicit treatment of consciousness as self-constituting in operational development, of development of meaning, and of development through differentiated self-conscious controls of meaning and value. In Lonergan's own words: "the power of methodical analysis is illustrated by its brevity."[52] Without going into details, several parallels with Insight may be drawn.

Lonergan proposed that mediation is more general than the notion of causality and, though materially a vague notion, can not only explicitate but also transpose Aristotelian nominal definition of immediate, mediate, and mediated terms based on causal necessity into implicit definition of functional relations and operations. In chapter one of Insight, the nominal, explanatory, and implicit types of definition are distinguished.[53]

Nominal definition merely specifies the correct usage of names, whereas explanatory definition supposes further determinations of the objects to which language refers.[54] An example given by Lonergan is the Euclidean definition of the circle: nominally, the circle is defined "as a perfectly round plane curve"; but explanatory definition affirms that "all radii in a circle are equal."[55] The explanatory definition asserts something more about the name 'cir-

----

[52]MoT, pp. 11-12.

[53]Insight, pp. 10-13. On definition, see Aristotle's Posterior Analytics, and I. Kant's Critique of Pure Reason, transl. by Norman Kempt Smith (New York: St. Martin's Press, Toronto: Mac Millan, 1929), pp. 314, 586-89. Lonergan's use of implicit definition will enable him to engage in immament rather than merely external critique envisioned by Kant. Immanent critique is common to the Hegelian-Marxist tradition (cf. n. 5 to ch. IV infra).

[54]Ibid., p. 11.

[55]Ibid.

cle'.

Implicit definition, worked out by Lonergan's teacher and friend, David Hilbert (1862-1943),[56] is the explanatory without the nominal definition. To give an example, one can derive the meaning of both the point and the straight line by establishing the relation "that two and only two points determine a straight line."[57] In implicit definition the terms fix the relations and the relations fix the terms, and the function fixes both.[58] Thus any mediate factor can be formally (functionally) determined as immediate in its source and mediated in the outcome.

To sum up: Nominal definitions mix descriptive and explanatory elements. Description expresses intelligible relations of things to us, whereas explanatory context considers intelligible relations of things to one another. A number of original Euclidean theorems remain unproved, while images are being used by Euclid in conjunction with nominal definitions to supply more than one can get out of axioms. Explanatory definitions work within imaginable limits, but implicit definitions eliminate these for the sake of strictly relational delimitations. David Hilbert rewrote Euclidean geometry on the basis of implicit definition and defined basic terms by their relations to one another and relations by the terms in the thus defined relations.

The notion of mediation, introduced in this chapter, is a more elaborate form of implicit definition: (1) It is an open pattern of structures, <u>invariant</u> in its general form. (2) It allows for enormous <u>variations</u> under differing limiting conditions. (3) It is subject to <u>differentiations</u>, and it <u>transcends</u> not only the imaginable but also those <u>limitations</u> of more primitive functions through the <u>displacement</u> and higher integration of the basic pattern of mediation. (4) It exhibits <u>isomorphism</u> of its gene-

---

[56]CAM, pp. 66-67.

[57]<u>Insight</u>, p. 12.

[58]Ibid.; in Lonergan's text: "[A]nd the insight fixes both," is his implicit, functional definition of understanding.

ral structure with variations, differentiations, higher integrations, and with categorial realizations of that general pattern, variations, differentiations, and higher integrations. I will now say something about each of the above points.

F i r s t , mediation is an invariant pattern of structures. The theorem states that any function of a factor is fixed immediately in the source and mediately in the outcome, and this will be true whether in the simple case of a watch, in the mutual mediation of a bodily functional whole, or the more complex self-mediation of genetic development. The invariance, then, lies in the set of recurrent operations, where any revison or transposition of the initial theorem does not alter the basic pattern of mediation.

Secondly, mediation allows for variations under differing limiting conditions. There can be variations in the same factor and variations of different factors within the same type of mediation. The movement of the watch, respiration, anger, or empirical science are examples of different functional wholes operating in a mutual mediation. For example, Fourier's function for the theory of heat will itself become a variable, and will function differently under differing limiting conditions. Or a chemical element, such as oxygen, is not a fixed nature but a variable mediated by a range of chemical transformations that will or will not combine under differing boundary conditions.

T h i r d l y , mediation is subject to further differentiations. Mutual mediation is differentiated from mediation in general by a cluster of immediate centers that enter into a functional whole. A body is a functional whole with centers of immediacy in the respiratory system, the digestive tract, the heart, or the nervous system. But mutual mediation cannot sufficiently account for genetic development. Besides growth of one cell to 2*n* cells, there are transitional and anticipatory developments, speciation and ecological interrelations. The transcendental function of development fixes the boundary conditions of mutual mediation. Thus, self-mediation by life, the displacement upwards by physical parts, consists in a higher integration of the basic pattern of mediation.

Fourthly, mediation exhibits isomorphism of its general pattern with variations, differentiations, higher integrations and their pertinent mediated realizations. 'Isomorphism' in Greek denotes 'equal' (*isos*) 'form' (*morphe*), hence, in Lonergan's usage, differentiation of and analogy to the basic pattern of mediation. This concept of isomorphism, as well as the set of related terms such as operation, transcendental function, limit, differentiation, integration, are taken from mathematical theory and its history. As a type of definition, mediation is, in Lonergan's words, "somewhat algebraic--it deals with x's and y's"; nevertheless, as a classification of development the notion of mediation transforms, preserves, and sublates the static character of classical logic and the fixed structures of Euclidean geometry.[59] To exemplify Lonergan's meaning of 'isomorphism', I will give a sketch of his treatment of mathematical history.

The transpositions from nominal to partially explanatory and fully explanatory implicit types of definition are isomorphic with the history of mathematical operations. This development is expressive of the shift from an imaginable context of description to abstract functional relations of explanation.

In his manuscript for the course on *Philosophy of Education*, Lonergan extrapolates from *L'idéal scientifique des mathématiciens* by Pierre Boutroux and points out three main scientific ideals of mathematics.[60] During the first period, the Greek mathematicians were concerned with geometrical objects, such as circles, ellipses, hyperbolas; or with numbers and their rational and irrational proportions. The second form of mathematical ideal, during the Renaissance period, represents a shift from the

---

[59]MoT, p. 96.

[60]Bernard Lonergan, *Philosophy of Education* (Cincinnati, Ohio: Xavier College, 1959), pp. 114-19; an unpublished, book-length manuscript is available from the Lonergan Institute, Regis College, Toronto. [Hereafter abbreviated as PE.]

geometric and numerical objects to the study of their genesis through differential calculus. The third is the contemporary ideal embodied in group theory. Contemporary mathematicians thus abstract both from the objects that interested the Greeks and the process of their genesis studied by the Renaissance thinkers, and they advert directly to human operations and their grouping.[61]

I will discuss briefly Lonergan's examples of isomorphism between these three periods. In the first place, Lonergan considers an analogy between proportion and the prolonged analogy of proportion, where the similarities (a whole) in relations are independent of what is related in the proportion (parts).[62] A numerical proportion, such as 4:14 :: 10:35, expresses an identity of partness and wholeness where the sign ':' refers to parts and the sign '::' refers to a whole. The ratio of a whole grounds the commensurability of its parts, i.e., given any two numbers, there is some number which is a measure of both. The ratio (logos) is 'sayable' of any intelligible proportionality.

The problem for the Greeks appeared with the discovery of incommensurable surds, e.g., the 'unsayable' (a-logos), the relations between a side of a square and its diagonal. 'Incommensurable' or 'irrational' "denies the possibility of applying to certain magnitudes some type of measurement . . . [and] a correspondence between certain numbers and human reason."[63] While a question such as "Why is a cartwheel round?" reveals a direct insight of intelligibility in the wheel, the answer to the question "Why is a surd a surd?" consists of what Lonergan calls inverse insight: The answer in the latter case "affirms empirical elements only to deny an expected intelligibility."[64]

----

[61]Ibid., pp. 114; 118.

[62]Bernard Lonergan, "Lectures On Mathematical Logic" (Boston: Boston College, July 1957), p. 5; an unpublished mimeographed transcript of these lectures is available from the Lonergan Institute, Regis College, Toronto. [Hereafter abbreviated as LML.]

[63]Insight, p. 20; cf. also p. 21.

Nevertheless, together with "a negative element indicated by the epithets, 'incommensurable,' 'irrational,'" there is also "a positive object indicated by terms 'magnitude,' 'number.'"[65] An inverse insight displaces not an intelligibility already reached (and amenable to further verification or falsification), but rather an intelligibility anticipated with one's questions. An inverse insight does not transform the positive content of the answers previously attained, but rather 'deconstructs' the negative, blind surd of the questions raised.[66] The very operation of 'deconstruction' (in Lonergan's sense) of the problematic context implies a mutual interdependence, an interplay of the positive and negative elements: "An inverse insight finds its expression only in some concomitant positive context."[67]

In the second place, "the same symbolic technique can provide a model for objects in series of isomorphic fields . . . for algebraic, geometrical, physical relations."[68] With the shift from proportions to functional thinking in the Renaissance the meaning of an expression which was previously signified either exclusively numerically or geometrically now itself becomes a variable meaning governed by a function that is derived from the solution to the differential equation. Thus it becomes possible to conceive of numbers geometrically and vice versa. Moreover, a limiting condition (boundary) of a function is itself a variable capable of further determinations, transformations, and differentiations by a function itself. This means that a variable fixed by a function comprises both the positive and negative significations, i.e., integrals (powers of correlations) and derivatives (differentiations).

Where previously the mathematician sought the unknown required number x, or the empirical enquirer

----

64Ibid., pp. 19-21.
65Ibid., p. 20 (italics mine).
66Cf. ibid., p. 19.
67Ibid., p. 24.
68LML. p. 5.

the unknown nature of *y*, now a differential equation of a form f(x,y,z . . .) = 0 will delimit the required function of *x* or *y* for both of them.[69] The difference between Aristotle and Galileo, says Lonergan, is that the former was "content to talk about the nature of light, the nature of heat, etc.," while the latter "inaugurated modern science by insisting that . . . from sensible similarity, which resides in the relations of things to our senses, one must proceed to relations that hold directly between things themselves."[70]

With A. Einstein's general theory of relativity, geometrical and space-time physical relations become themselves unknown variable functional systems operating differently under differing conditions.[71] Einstein's postulate of *invariance*, relativity, states that certain classes of differential equations will not undergo "change in the form despite changes in spatio-temporal standpoint," i.e., they are invariant under a specified group of transformations.[72] The meaning signified by a variable of space-time relations comprises both the positive and negative expression:

> [T]he difference between the anticipations represented respectively by General and by Special Relativity is that, while both expect invariant mathematical expression to result from the abstractness of principles and laws, General Relativity implements this expectation by invoking a *direct insight* into the significance of measurement but Special Relativity implements it by invoking an *inverse insight* into the significance of constant velocity.[73]

----

[69]*Insight*, pp. 36-8.

[70]Ibid., p. 38.

[71]On General Relativity see *Insight*, pp. 39-46 and the index there under "Relativity."

[72]Ibid., p. 40.

[73]Ibid., p. 42 (italics mine).

In the third place, besides isomorphism between geometrical, algebraic and space-time relations, one can think of mathematics in terms of operations expressed in group theory.[74] First, the operations may be physical, such as drawing a circle on the blackboard; or intermediate, when operating with the symbols; or remote, as upon the symbols themselves.[75] Whereas the symbolic operations can serve as models for the total range of logical relations in mathematical logic, symbolic logic, and logistics,[76] Lonergan's notion of mediation transposes the merely logical relations into functional ones which are capable of generating any other type of relations in the series of isomorphic fields: mechanical, organic, psychic, cognitional, ethical, economic, spiritual, etc.

The application of mathematical terminology to mediation also takes on the 'equal form': invariants pertain to the basic structure of mediation, differentiations play a role that is isomorphic to the one of differential equations in solving a function, transcendental functions enable operations to go beyond the boundary conditions of the lower to higher integrations, and the mediated realizations admit the same type of transpositions of the basic operations as do those between geometry, algebra, and the space-time relations.

Finally, an introduction of group theory into mathematics engenders, in Lonergan's words,

> an entirely different approach to a science; it is in terms of the operations of the scientist as distinct from the formal object. . . .
> . . . .
> [For] mathematics is not the science of quantity, but the science of intelligible groups and relations in quantity. . . .

----

[74]PE, pp. 117ff.
[75]Ibid.
[76]LML, p. 5.

> . . . .
> If one thinks of a group of operations as constituting a science, then the division and integration of the sciences becomes a matter of division and integration of groups of operations. And human history, the history that is written about, becomes the totality of human operations.[77]

(2) Structuralism, deconstruction, and Lonergan's notion of mediation as a dynamic structure

An introduction of group theory into methods of investigation engenders not only "an entirely different approach to a science and the human history that is written about," but also inaugurates a type of 'deconstruction' of different human discourses in terms of their development through various operations. In the preceeding section I have discussed the basic and derived terms of a dynamic structure of mediation and their differentiation in isomorphic fields of human operations. I will now relate the second aspect of Lonergan's methodological analysis, namely, an expansion of a dynamic structure of mediation through operational development. I will clarify: first, Lonergan's treatment of structuralist methodology; and, secondly, a sense in which both J. Derrida and Lonergan go beyond structuralism, but differ in their post-structuralist project of _deconstruction_.

In his lecture on structuralism and hermeneutics, Lonergan compares his treatment of a dynamic structure with the concerns for unconscious, deep structures in human beings as found among the tenets of the structuralist movements.[78] Here is how Lonergan links his earlier exposition of implicit definition in _Insight_ with some findings of linguistic structuralism:

----

[77]PE, pp. 117, 127, 118.
[78]WCLS, p. 6.

> [Structuralism] is a linguistic theory that considers a language as a structured set where all terms are defined by their mutual relations. And in that connection you can think of Hilbert's rewriting of Euclid's geometry. . . . So that a point need not mean something with position but without length, breadth and thickness. It could mean an ordered pair or an ordered triad or an ordered quartet of numbers; and a straight line would mean a first degree equation without any image added on and so on. It is a way of eliminating the images and consequently eliminating the fallacies that are involved in the Euclidean presentation of geometry.[79]

The key point made by a Swiss linguist, Ferdinand de Saussure, in his analysis of language is, says Lonergan, that he considers words in their relations to one another and apart from their relations to objects.[80] The standard example of this high formalism and abstraction is the dictionary: "[A]ny word in the dictionary is also explained in the dictionary; it forms a closed circle--the words alone apart from the things they are talking about. . . ."[81] Both in structuralism and in the English variety of linguistic philosophy, Lonergan clarifies, one arrives at the meaning of human signs by knowing their usage within a known context. The first works on linguistic structuralism "showed that each language is a particular system of pure differences, a totality of signs in which it is the whole that endows with meaning each of the parts."[82]

F. de Saussure thematized these 'pure differences' of language in the binary relation between a

----

[79]Ibid.
[80]Ibid.
[81]Ibid., p. 2.
[82]Ibid.

signifier (sound-image) and the signified (the meant). One's meaning (signification) is based on the context and use-relation of a sign to the signified. Other types of binary relations, most treated by a Czech formalist, Roman Jakobson and a French ethnologist Claude Lévi-Strauss, are the metaphor-metonymy and synchrony-diachrony. The former pair distinguishes between language in primitive, timeless, mythopoeic culture and the one in modern culture, dominated by the space-time causality of correlation and contiguity. The latter pair differentiates between the horizontal axis of simultaneous objects within synchronic (circular) time and the vertical axis of successive objects within diachronic (linear) time.[83]

To give a general definition, structuralism attempts to uncover deep, universal mental structures in language, literature, mathematics, music, philosophy, and in unconscious patterns that generate human behavior in various primitive and developed cultures. Since the 'deep structures' sought-for by the structuralists in different branches of inquiry--psychoanalytic, formalist, existentialist, thematic, Marxist--are presumed to be unconscious, these cannot be verified directly.[84] Moreover, in Edith Kurzweil's evaluation of the state of the structuralist current of thought:

> [S]tructuralism as originally conceived by Lévi-Strauss is dead: the universal mental structures have not emerged, albeit no one any longer searches for them. . . . Thus, the failure of Parisian structuralism itself has prepared the ground for the various "post-structuralisms."[85]

Lonergan is not a structuralist, at least not in

----

[83]Ibid., pp. 7, 14.

[84]Ibid., p. 7, 21.

[85]Edith Kurzweil, The Age of Structuralism: Lévi-Strauss to Foucault (New York: Columbia University Press, 1980), p. 10.

any sense in which the movement has been conceived and carried on. The point of his lecture on Levi-Strauss is to specify how his own analysis in part fulfils the promise, but mostly transposes the original project of structuralism by explicating the basic and derived group of operations of the structuralist as a human subject. This is one of the common grounds, on which Derrida and Lonergan engage in a project of a post-structuralist 'deconstruction'. The differences between them, however, loom large. I will now sketch Derrida's meaning of deconstruction and then compare it with Lonergan's sublation of structuralism into his own method.

G. D. Atkins offers a clue to the meaning of Derrida's deconstruction: its meaning is bound to the latter's "undoing/ preserving of the concept of the sign central to modern linguistics."[86] According to Saussure the link between the signifier and the signified is a wholly external and arbitrary relationship, which is made possible by a structure of pure differences inherent in distinct phonic and graphic aspects of signs themselves. Derrida, on the other hand, indicates that in the binary nexus of the signifier/signified, "the sign is that ill-named thing, the only one that escapes the instituting question of philosophy: 'What is . . . ?'"[87] Derrida deconstructs the differential character of language signs--assigned to them by Western preoccupations with a "metaphysics of presence"--by putting the binary oppositions, such as the signifier/signified, presence/ absence, mind/body, good/evil, master/slave, identity/difference, speech/ writing, literature/criticism, being/nothingness, etc., "under erasure." He writes a word, e.g. 'Being', crosses it out, and prints both; for, as Atkins comments, "though the word is inaccurate it is necessary and must remain legible."[88]

----

[86]Douglas G. Atkins, Reading Deconstruction Deconstructive Reading (Kentucky: The University Press of Kentucky, 1983), p. 16.

[87]Jacques Derrida, Of Grammatology, trans. by Gayatri Chakravorty Spivak (Baltimore: John Hopkins University Press, 1976), p. 20.

[88]Atkins, op. cit., pp. 17, 20. Cf. Jacques

MEDIATION AS A DYNAMIC STRUCTURE

Derrida's project of deconstructive erasure of the above oppositions finds its embodiment in a newly coined French term la différance (from différer, means both to differ and to defer), by which, according to B. Johnson, Derrida expresses the "lag inherent in any signifying act," because "to mean . . . is automatically not to be. As soon as there is meaning, there is difference."[89] Derrida's use of la différance (do not confuse it with la différence, an equivalent of English difference) effects a critique of Western metaphysics through a deconstruction of (1) any privilege of the spoken over the written word, (2) various philosophies of 'presence' stated either in a univocal determination of Being as presence, or in what he calls a logocentric desire of an immediate self-presence of meaning in structures of human consciousness and unconsciousness, or in the Hegelian dialectic of identity, and of (3) various written discourses for the sake of displacing the claims "to unequivocal domination of one mode of signifying over another."[90]

The program of deconstruction, however, attempts not destruction but analysis, 'un-doing' of all logocentric and metaphysical claims in any text; as Johnson sums up: "the deconstructive reading does not point out the flaws or weaknessess or stupidities of an author, but the necessity with which what he does see is systematically related to what he does not see."[91] To specify the three points mentioned above: Derrida's différance shows, first, that the

---

Derrida, Dissemination, trans., with an Introduction and notes, by Barbara Johnson (Chicago: University of Chicago Press, 1981), see an example of Derrida's 'erasure' of Being on p. 354.

[89]Derrida, Dissemination, introduction by B. Johnson, p. ix. Note that differance is a new word coined by Derrida.

[90]Ibid., pp. viii-xiv; the cited text is on p. xiv. Cf. Vincent Descombes, Modern French Philosophy, trans. by L. Scott-Fox and J. M. Harding (Cambridge: Cambridge University Press, 1980); see ch. 5 on "Difference," pp. 136-152.

[91]Ibid., pp. xiv-xv.

possibility of the signifier's role depends upon a deferral (lag) into the future of any presencing of the thing itself; i.e., deferral of Saussure's 'phonocentric' differential character of language structure. According to Norris, "where Derrida breaks new ground . . . is in the extent to which 'differ' shades into 'defer'. This involves the idea that meaning is always _deferred_, perhaps to the point of an endless supplementarity, by the play of signification."[92]

Secondly, _différance_ produces deconstructive reading and a strategy of writing that, says Derrida, dislocates both the author's and one's own assumptions of originative presence either as thematized in a metaphysics of being, or in a phenomenology of identity, or in various theories of structuralism:

> Without the possibility of différance, the desire of presence as such would not find its breathing space. That means by the same token that this desire carries in itself a destiny of its nonsatisfaction. Différance produces what it forbids, making possible the very thing that it makes impossible.[93]

Hence, Derrida's deconstruction of Western metaphysics, and of Hegel's _Aufhebung_ in particular, remains interminable; it is itself an embodiment of _différance_

> between philosophy, which is always a philosophy of presence, and a meditation on non-presence--which is not perforce its contrary, or necessarily a meditation on a negative absence, or a theory of non-

----

[92]Christopher Norris, _Deconstruction: Theory and Practice_ (London, New York: Methuen, 1982), p. 32.

[93]Derrida, _Of Grammatology_, p.143; quoted by Johnson in Derrida, _Dissemination_, pp. xi-xii.

presence *qua* unconsciousness.[94]

Thirdly, *différance* expresses a rift between an unequivocal domination of a phenomenological structure over a structuralist mode of signifying, and vice versa. Derrida specifies this mutual displacement of phenomenology and structuralism: "in every proposition or in every system of semiotic research . . . metaphysical propositions coexist with critical motifs."[95] Deconstruction as a form of displacement of the starting-point concealed in any theoretical system exhibits phenomenological, critical aspects; nevertheless, the project of analysis is primarily an activity performed by the texts and their differential-deferrential structures. This rift is characterized in Derrida's remark: "What I can never understand, in a structure, is that by means of which it is not closed."[96] Deconstruction thus surpasses 'structure' by relating genesis of meaning and logocentrism of criticism through a mutual displacement of the assumed origination of meaning in the author. Norris sums up the point:

> Structuralism itself arises from the break with an attitude (the phenomenological) it cannot reject but must perpetually put in question. . . . Structuralism and phenomenology are locked in a reciprocal *aporia* from which neither can emerge with its principles intact, but on which both depend for

----

[94]Jacques Derrida, *Speech and Phenomena: And Other Essays on Husserl's Theory of Signs*, trans. by David B. Allison (Evanston, Ill.: Northwestern University Press, 1973), p. 170; cited by Descombes, *op. cit*., p. 149.

[95]Jacques Derrida, *Positions* trans. by Alan Bass (London: Athlone Press, 1981), p. 36; cited by Norris, *op. cit*., p. 48; see also pp. 48-55 in Norris.

[96]Jacques Derrida, *Writing and Difference*, trans. by Alan Bass (London: Routledge and Kegan Paul, 1978), p. 160; cited by Norris, *op. cit*., p. 54.

their moments of maximum insight.[97]

But it is precisely this aporia, mentioned above by Norris, that will supply Lonergan's argument and engender--instead of the mutual displacement characteristic of Derrida's project of deconstruction--mediation through a series of displacements in human operational development.

I will return now to Lonergan's paper on structuralism. He points out that structures as such do not exhibit in themselves the marks of process and genesis, though it is possible to speak of "genetic structures and constant procedures of production."[98] He will side with the genetic structuralism of Piaget (over, e.g. Noam Chomsky), who delimits structuralism to a method rather than a doctrine. For Piaget structure and genesis are interdependent in such a manner that no structure functions apart from construction.[99] It is in Piaget's sense that Lonergan characterizes the performance of the structuralist; his work is to

> recover the rules governing the appropriate use of signs; one reconstructs the signs by placing them in the context of their usage, their functioning; the reconstructing is a developed understanding of the sign. . . . You know the meaning of the word if you know how to use it. Your reconstructing yields a developed understanding of the sign.[100]

The performance consists then of a reconstruction or reconstitution of the original work as opposed to a type of criticism that leads to a mere "refabrication . . . for the sake of a copy. .. ."[101] The reconstruction yields a developed understanding

----

[97]Norris, op. cit., p. 51.
[98]WCLS, p. 22.
[99]Kurzweil, op. cit., introduction, n. 1.
[100]WCLS, p. 7.
[101]Ibid.

of "a homology, an analogy of functions, between the original and its reconstitution."[102] The analogy sought for is not, however, merely between the original work and its structuralist analysis, but also between the structuralist's knowing and performance. One's understanding is itself analogous to the content of the structuralist's critique. This analogy pertains not to structuralism as a school or a movement, but rather to "an activity, a regulated succession of mental operations."[103] Just as in the history of mathematics Lonergan discerned the movement from the mathematics of proportions to functional and operational thinking, so here he draws a parallel between structuralism as a theory and the operations that generate it as such a theory. With regard to theoretical structuralism, Lonergan is a 'post-structuralist'; in the sense in which he accounts for the praxis of structuralism, he grounds that possibility in terms of the structuralist's own 'cognitional structure', "in which all the terms are operations . . . and the relation is the dynamism relating one operation on to the next."[104]

Lonergan's reconstruction of the structuralist's use of signs thus yields a 'deconstruction' of structuralism as a theory. The rift between the two emerges in an opposition of the structuralist's search for the originating deep mental structures to what is left out unthematized as the cognitional dynamism of this search itself. The _aporia_ between phenomenology and structuralism, of which Norris spoke above, takes the central place in Lonergan's analysis of open cognitional structure, i.e., operational development which I will take up in Part Two.

To borrow G. Aichele's definition of deconstruction and to apply it to Lonergan's methodology:

> To deconstruct is to take apart what has been contructed, to find a point of assembly in terms of which the entire construction becomes

----

[102]Ibid.
[103]Ibid., p. 6.
[104]Ibid.

> possible, and which is therefore simultaneously "inside" and "outside" of the constructed . . . to find the incompleteness in every systematic illusion of completeness, the non-being at the heart of being, the sign in terms of which all other signs in the significant system are defined but which itself eludes all definition.[105]

Lonergan's 'deconstruction' of various human discourses leads to a point of assembly--which is not a point but an implicit definition thereof--mediated through a series of displacements in human operational development. His is a 'deconstruction upwards',i.e., through one's appropriation of self-mediating functions. For it is the function that can comprise both its variable differentiating, and integrative aspects--and thus be simultaneously 'inside' and 'outside' of the constructed. Such an approach inaugurates not only an entirely different account of a science and of history that is written about, but it "is also relevant for solving [which equals 'deconstructing', sublating, and mediating] such problems as the construction of a Catholic philosophy."[106]

Derrida's _différance_ comes into play in Lonergan's canon of residues for a methodical hermeneutics. 'Deconstruction' of the blind alleys of questioning (the negative of inverse insight), however, does not operate apart from its positive context:

> Just as the field of physics contains a non-systematic component, so also do the fields of

----

[105]Georg Aichele Jr., "Hegel and Deconstruction," _Cross Currents_ Vol. 34, No. 1 (Spring 84), p. 119; this is a book review of Mark C. Taylor's _Deconstructing Theology_ (New York: Crossroad, 1982).

[106]PE, pp. 115, 117, 118.

> meaning, of expression as related to meaning, of expression as grounded in dynamic constellations of the writer's psyche, and of documents in their origins, their production, and their survival. Just as the physicist deals with the non-systematic by combining inverse with direct insights, so also must the interpreter.[107]

The non-systematic, which eludes direct definition, is characterized by Lonergan as the 'protean' (shifting, variable) notion of being; and it finds a specific form in "the recurrent gap between meaning and expression."[108] Now if one views the 'systematic' as corresponding to the work of an electronic computer, then the only acceptable system is a static one.[109] On the other hand, if human meaning and expression originate within a system on the move, then the non-systematic in the work of interpretation or investigation can be defined "as differentiating the protean notion of being."[110]

The two senses of deconstruction can now be compared. First, if for Derrida, *differance* means a deconstruction of Western logocentrism and metaphysics of presence, Lonergan accounts for the gap between meaning and expression by inverse insight into the intelligibility of the non-systematic.

Secondly, if Derrida's deconstruction of the Hegelian reconciliation between the subject and object in the self-presence of Absolute Spirit remains an interminable interplay of the signifiers (*differance* is not a negation of Hegel's dialectic of identity), Lonergan partly accepts Hegelian *Aufhebung*, but he also applies it to Hegel's thought itself.[111] Lonergan accepts the Hegelian movement to higher

----

[107]*Insight*, pp. 590-91.

[108]Ibid., p. 589; see the index there under "Being."

[109]Ibid., p. 591; also 388.

[110]Ibid., p. 592.

[111]Cf. Ibid., pp. 374, 422.

viewpoints, and even thematizes a possibility of the universal viewpoint, which 'deconstructs', sublates, and retains previous levels of intelligibility, but he sublates Hegel's contention that mediation "has to pretend to be complete independently of non-systematic matters of fact."[112]

Thirdly, while Derrida's deconstruction reduces human discourses to an ahistorical, intertextual interplay of signifiers, and thus forsakes both their authors and speakers, Lonergan effects a 'deconstruction' of (an inverse insight into) the perennial questions about reality, truth, objectivity, and the good. The former would deny that deconstruction is a subject matter or a methodology; rather, "the movements of deconstruction do not destroy structures from outside. . . . Operating necessarily from the inside . . . the enterprise of deconstruction always in a certain way falls prey to its own work."[113] The latter conceives 'method' not as a set of rules to be followed blindly; method is not a technique "as in the assembly line or 'The New Method Laundry.'"[114] Lonergan's 'deconstruction' also operates from within, but what it falls prey to is its own development. For Lonergan, "evidence does not lie in the outward vocal or written expression"; nor is the evidence a 'Lonerganian' (or for that matter Aristotelian, Kantian, Transcendental-Thomist, Piagetian, etc.) argument produced by a book (of his or his commentators) to be simply assented to, but rather an advance through "an invitation to a personal, decisive act,"--one's appropriation of the positive and negative aspects of one's dynamic, protean structure of operational development.[115] Thus, it is true to state that Lonergan's enterprise is one of 'deconstruction' insofar as it does not

----

[112]Ibid., p. 594.

[113]Derrida, Of Grammatology, p. 24; cited by Carl A. Raschke, "The Deconstruction of God," in J. J. Thomas Alitzer, et al., Deconstruction and Theology (New York: Crossroad, 1982), p. 10.

[114]Bernard Lonergan, Method In Theology (New York: Herder & Herder, 1972), pp. 5-6. [Hereafter abbreviated as MIT.]

[115]Insight, pp. 484, xix, 396.

belong to any school of '-isms' or '-ologies', and as far as it falls prey to its own protean interplay of mediation.

Fourthly, Derrida plays the 'double game' of using and erasing the signs that express human desire of unmediated presence, such as 'is'; whereas Lonergan thematizes the opposition between the pure desire to know and the interference of alien desires which can block human understanding or foster bias. While Derrida's deconstruction falls prey to its own interminable displacement of intelligibility, Lonergan's 'falls prey' to displacement of flight from understanding for the sake of interminable creativity of intelligence. Derrida's deconstruction of the apparently systematic, permanent, and differential character of written discourse leads to a triple displacement of the 'transcendental signified': God, the human subject, and human history. On the other hand, Lonergan reverses the questions that lead to a systematization of common nonsense in common misunderstanding not by a liquidation of the departments of human, natural and theological inquiries, but through "the reorientation demanded and effected by the self-knowledge of the subject."[116] If Derrida puts written expressions of the desire of unmediated presence "under erasure," then Lonergan's 'deconstruction', besides the process of displacement of naive immediacy, also sublates and mediates that alien desire (which he names an animal one) through a threefold intellectual, moral, and religious conversion engendered by development into human authenticity. What is meant by 'conversion' should become clearer as the reader proceeds through later chapters of this study.

I will conclude with a summary account of the reorientation of human inquiry envisioned in Lonergan's description of methods of investigation.

(3) The classical, statistical, genetic and dialectical methods of investigation

If we return to the general notion of mediation,

----

[116]Ibid., p. 399; also p. 422.

then different modes of its protean pattern can be put in the following types of isomorphic questions: What is the operation of the movement in the watch? What is the watch 'performing' when it is measuring time? What is the body doing when it breathes, digests, circulates blood, and controls all these immediate centers of operations? What is the body doing when it grows and reproduces itself? What is the function operative in the development of the species? What is the natural scientist doing when operating empirically and scientifically? What am I doing when I am knowing? Why is doing that knowing? What do I know when I am operating as knower? These questions are isomorphic with respect to the intelligibility anticipated and in the sense that they exhibit the basic pattern of mediation. Nevertheless, the answers are subject both to the variations of different types of investigation that each question calls for, and to differentiations in the source as well as in the affirmed outcome of a problem-solution.

The underlying positive and negative aspects of the isomorphism pertaining to the above questions is Plato's Meno paradox, stated by Lonergan as follows: "But how can means be ordered to an end when the end is knowledge and the knowledge is not yet acquired?"[117] Lonergan's reply to the Meno unifies the strategic application of mediation to varying methods of investigation: "The answer to this puzzle is the heuristic structure. Name the unknown. Work out its properties. Use the properties to direct, order, guide the inquiry."[118] This heuristic strategy of inquiry from the known, through the known unknown, to the unknown unknown yields results analogical to a work of a physicist who "unites a differential equation with empirically ascertained boundary conditions, to obtain the integral heuristic structure relevant to this universe."[119]

The basic pattern of inquiry, a heuristic infra-

----

[117]Ibid., p. 44; cf. Plato, the Meno, Stephanus n. 80d.

[118]Ibid. (italics mine).

[119]Ibid., p. 484.

structure, is fixed by the dynamic function of immediate, mediate, and mediated terms in cognitional structure, namely by experience, understanding, judgment, and deliberation. But there are different types of investigation in which this basic pattern of operations expands. In pre-scientific, e.g., Aristotelian thought, the intelligible similarity anticipated in all similar data is named the "nature of."[120] Modern science anticipates correlations of functions within a fully explanatory context. Lonergan distinguishes in Insight the classical, statistical, genetic, and dialectical methods of investigation. [Figure 1.]

Classical method "heads towards the determinations of functions and their systematization. . . . [C]lassical conclusions are concerned with what would be if other things were equal. . . ."[121] A type of heuristic mediation under a classical investigation will anticipate "the systematic-and-abstract on which the concrete converges."[122] The statistical investigation treats what is considered as the non-systematic and unintelligible under the classical laws. It will anticipate "the systematic-and-abstract setting a boundary or norm from which the concrete cannot systematically diverge."[123] What the classical investigator prescinds from and what remains under classical laws unintelligible (incommensurable) is now the subject of the statistical laws expressed in an intelligible function "of the non-systematic aggregate of patterns of diverging series of conditions."[124] Both types of inquiry are complementary:

> [E]xact and complete knowledge of classical laws cannot successfully invade the field of statistical laws; and statistical investigations are confronted with regular recurrences that admit

----

[120]Ibid., p. 44.
[121]Ibid., p. 53 (italics mine).
[122]Ibid., p. 103.
[123]Ibid.
[124]Ibid., p. 114.

> explanations of the classical type.[125]

Further, development that remains under both classical and statistical laws unintelligible becomes the subject of genetic method, which studies sequences of related systems, and dialectical method that is concerned with the relations between successive sequences of changing systems. Different types of questions yield different angles of the anticipations of intelligibility: systematic, diverging from systems in schemes of recurrence, probabilities of emergence, survival and decline of a single scheme.[126] As the direct insight leads to foundations of intelligible laws, so the inverse insight discovers and 'deconstructs' the defective intelligibility:

> [T]he anticipation of a constant system to be discovered grounds classical method; the anticipation of an intelligibly related sequence of systems grounds genetic method; the anticipation that data will not conform to system grounds statistical method; and the anticipation that relations between successive stages of changing system will not be directly intelligible grounds dialectical method. . . [T]aken together, *the four methods are relevant to any field of data; they do not dictate what data must be; they are able to cope with data no matter what they prove to be*.[127]

It will suffice for our purposes, without going into Lonergan's account of emergent probability, to point out the invariants, variables, differentiations, transcendental functions, and isomorphisms of the generalized empirical notion of heuristic mediation, i.e., what pertains to the generalized empi-

---

[125]Ibid., p. 115.
[126]Ibid., pp. 117-18.
[127]Ibid., p. 485 (italics mine).

rical method comprising the four types of inquiry described above. Invariants are expanded in variations of classical and statistical laws. Variations yield to systems, divergences from systems, schemes of recurrence, and differentiations of emergent probability. The limitations of classical investigation are transcended in statistical method; the limitations of either classical or statistical laws are transcended in a complementary investigation of probabilities. The limitations of probabilities as applied to self-mediation of living organisms require further differentiation in genetic method of investigation anticipating the intelligibility of development. Genetic method as applied to human beings consists of a threefold consideration of development: organic, psychic, and existential.

Finally, dialectical method will differentiate between a _basic position_ and a _basic counter-position_ in any philosophical formulation of self-mediation through various methods of inquiry as these have appeared in historical development of human understanding.[128] For in any philosophical performance one can distinguish between its _basis_ in cognitional theory and its _expansion_ in pronouncements "on any epistemological, metaphysical, ethical, or theological" issues.[129] Dialectical method adverts to the _polymorphic fact_ of human consciousness and differentiates the protean notion of being "by a set of genetically and dialectically related determinations."[130] A basic counter-position determines the _real_ as the "already-out-there-now," _knowing_ as analogical to ocular vision, _objectivity_ as a matter of elementary anticipation, animal extroversion and satisfaction, and the _good_ as what is simply given or immediately apprehensible in the structures of natural law.[131] The evidence for a basic position proceeds from a 'deconstruction', a reversal brought about by a counter-position itself: "The only coherent way to maintain a counter-position is that of an animal; for animals not only do not speak but also

---

[128]Cf. ibid., p. 387.
[129]Ibid., p. 388.
[130]Ibid., p. 581.
[131]Cf. ibid., pp. 388, 581-82.

do not offer excuses for their silence."[132] The evidence furnished in a 'deconstruction' of the historical series of philosophies comprises the _positive aspect_ that justifies their contribution to human development and the _negative aspect_ that accounts for their breakdown and reversal.[133] To thematize this process of mediation between the basic and expanded group of operations will be the task undertaken in Part Two.

I assumed with Lonergan that classical, statistical, and genetic investigations are isomorphic in the general pattern of mediation they employ as they anticipate intelligibility in the world. But as Lonergan had to prescind from organism _qua_ living in treating mutual mediation until he was dealing with self-mediation by life development, so he had to prescind from operational development of human beings until he was dealing directly with self-mediation of conscious operations.[134] If Lonergan's notion of mediation is his transposition of both Aristotelian and Hegelian logic, and of their respective philosophies of nature, then self-mediation by operational development is his transposition of both Hegel's and contemporary phenomenology's self-mediation. The two parts of this study exemplify a division in accord with the above transpositions. The reader should note that nothing has yet been said about a basic position (derived from the basic heuristic infrastructure of experience, understanding, judgment, and deliberation) to be appropriated through the dialectical method of investigation. Without jumping to the conclusions of Lonergan's argument, I may say that the basic and expanded pattern of the world-view to which he concludes will be isomorphic with the methodological notion of mediation that this chapter invoked.

----

[132]Ibid., p. 388.

[133]Ibid., p. 389.

[134]Note Lonergan's comment in section on "Genetic Method": "But while we employed genetic method in outlining the development of mathematics, of natural science, and of common sense, still we were forced to refrain from explaining what precisely we were doing." [_Insight_, p. 458.]

MEDIATION AS A DYNAMIC STRUCTURE

PROTEAN NOTION of MEDIATION: BASE----EXPANSION

Mediation	Base	Expansion
Mediation in General (F= any factor, property, quality, aspect, feature.)	source, origin, ground.	outcome derivatives consequences expression a field of influence
Mutual Mediation (F1--F2)= any functional whole constituted by mutually mediating parts.	different centers of immediacy (F1), (F2), . . .	F<whole>= [(F1)(F2)]
Self-mediation: living Any whole with consequences that change the whole.	different functional wholes.	growth/anticipatory and transitory development/ speciation/ displacement upwards
classical laws	any regular function.	any system of functions.
statistical laws variable systems operating under variable space-time conditions.	non-systematic schemes of recurrence/probabilities of emergence and survival/ decline of a single or a series of schemes of recurrence.	
genetic laws variable, organic, psychic and existential systems operating under variable organic, psychic and existential conditions.		flexible sequence of schemes of development according to successive application of the principle of correspondence and emergence.
Self-mediation: methods of investigation in operational development.	basic group of operations in cognitional structure anticipating systematic, non-systematic and developmental intelligibility.	pronouncements on common sense/ science/ philosophy scholarship/ and and theology.
Dialectical method of investigation	a basic position or counter-position on the real, known, objective and good.	'deconstruction' of basic counter-positions and development through self-appropriation of a basic position

Figure 1. Mediation: basic and derived terms

PART TWO:

SELF-MEDIATION: OPERATIONAL DEVELOPMENT

I think that, with respect to the relation of Western Europe to the totalitarian systems, no error could be greater than the one looming largest--that of a failure to understand the totalitarian systems for what they ultimately are, a convex mirror of all modern civilization and a harsh, perhaps the final call for a global recasting of that civilization's self-understanding.

The slogan, "better red than dead," does not irritate me as an expression of surrender to the Soviet Union, but it terrifies me as an expression of the resignation of western humans of any claim to a meaningful life and of their acceptance of impersonal power as such.

Václav Havel, "Politika a svědomí," Svědectví: Czechoslovak Quarterly Review XVIII, No. 72 (Paris: Tigrid, 1984): 621-35.

If the world has not approached its end, it has reached a major watershed in history, equal in importance to the turn from the Middle Ages to the Renaissance. It will demand from us a spiritual blaze; we shall have to rise to a new height of vision, to a new level of life, where our physical nature will not be cursed, as in the Middle Ages, but even more importantly, our spiritual being will not be trampled upon, as in the Modern Era.

This ascension is similar to climbing unto the next anthropological stage. No one on earth has any other way left but--upward.

Aleksandr I. Solzshenitsyn, A World Split Apart, Commencement Address Delivered at Harvard University June 8, 1978. (New York: Harper & Row, 1978), pp. 59-61.

Introduction

In the first chapter I have laid the ground for the main argument of this study, namely, Lonergan's use of mediation in his methodological analysis of human operational development. Three types of mediation were considered: the general notion of mediation, mutual mediation, and self-mediation through the living of organisms. The limitations of mutual mediation--of a functional whole--were transcended in organic self-mediation by a displacement upwards of physical parts. Besides the classical and statistical methods of investigation, genetic method was needed to deal with the new factor of development: "Genetic method is concerned with sequences in which correlations and regularities change . . . with a sequence of operators that successively generate functions from an initial function."[1]

The term operator is taken from a mathematical analogy: an operator in mathematics changes one function into another.[2] The operator differs from the integrator. The latter corresponds to a set of functional wholes under the guidance of both classical and statistical laws. The former effects "the transition from one set of forms, laws, schemes to another set."[3] Again, the integrator exhibits the "principle of correspondence" of all achieved integrations within the stage and the limits in development.[4] The operator effects the novel higher integrations according to the "principle of emergence."[5]

Lonergan illustrates in Insight this interaction between the integrator and operator by three examples of self-mediating development. First, by a biological study of development of a fossil. The biologist can reconstruct the organism of a dinosaur by examining its organic parts, such as the bones. The simultaneous interlocking of the parts with one another exhibits the whole of the integrator.[6] On the other

----

[1]Insight, p. 461.
[2]Ibid., p. 465.
[3]Ibid.; on operator-integrator, see pp.464-67, 476-77.
[4]Ibid., pp. 451-452.
[5]Ibid.
[6]Ibid., p. 465.

hand, a successive interlocking of parts over time reveals not only "a determinate stage in the development of the whole," but also earlier and later stages from which "the higher system as operator" can be inferred.[7]

Secondly, the fact that "a tree in a forest puts forth branches and leaves not to its sides but at its top" specifies the function of the operator as "the higher system on the move," and, at the same time, the biologist's grasp of the operator "begins to be an instance of higher system on the move in the development of scientific knowledge of development."[8] The intelligible in genetic laws of development yields in the scientist to the intelligent development of various methods of investigation--the one type of development mediates the higher system on the move that in this case is an intelligently operating researcher.

Thirdly, in human development, genuineness frees one's admission into consciousness of the tension between one's limitation and one's ideal self, i.e., between a "solid and salutary conservatism" of the integrator and the relentless exigence towards self-transcendence of the operator.[9] Genuineness is one's creative response to the tension between the unconscious and conscious aspects of human development.[10] The opposite of the conservatism Lonergan has here in mind is not a naive liberalism, but rather one's development towards authentic freedom. Hence, the operator grounds what has come to be known as the reflective--over and above the merely logical and acquisitive--function of reason. Genuineness is the catalyst of human development towards freedom which displaces the naïveté of both one-dimensional conservatism and the immediate gratification of extroverted activism of the liberal. The argument developed in

----

[7]Ibid.

[8]Ibid., p. 467.

[9]Ibid., p. 477.

[10]Ibid., pp. 476, 478. See also Jeremiah L. Alberg, S.J. "The Notion of Genuineness in Bernard Lonergan's Insight," M.A. Thesis (St. Louis University, 1981).

the chapters that follow will move along the lines of authentic freedom.

Self-mediation was characterized as a functional whole "that has consequences that change the whole."[11] Self-mediation is a _self-constituting_ functional whole. In living organisms self-constitution is effected by development of physical parts, by reproduction, speciation, ecological inter-relations;[12] but in human development a higher type of self-constituting functional whole emerges: self-mediation by consciousness--_displacement inwards_.[13]

Moreover, the self-constituting functions of consciousness are constitutive of further mediations: (1) operational development in adaptation, grouping, cognitive, constitutive, effective, and communicative functions of meaning; (2) differentiated controls of meaning and value; (3) self-mediation towards self-conscious autonomy and genuine freedom--_deliberate shift of center_; and (4) mutual self-mediation as a combination of mutual mediation and self-mediation in the human encounters of all different communitarian and historical life worlds. There is possible, then, a fourfold consideration of conscious development towards human autonomy: First, consciousness as self-constituting; secondly, consciousness as mediated and constituted by meaning; thirdly, consciousness as differentiated from common sense and mythic controls of meaning: theoretical, critical, and transcendental controls; and fourthly, consciousness as self-constituting of controls and differentiations in mediation by the methodical exigence of meaning and value. The first two considerations will be taken up in chapters II and III; the latter two will be treated in chapter IV.

----

[11]MCP, p. 6.
[12]Ibid., p. 2.
[13]Ibid.

CHAPTER II

CONSCIOUSNESS AS SELF-CONSTITUTING

In his lecture "Time and Meaning,"[14] delivered in Montreal in the Fall of 1962, and during the summer institute on "Method of Theology" (Toronto, 1962), Lonergan linked his earlier analysis of development in the chapter on Genetic Method in Insight with "a more detailed account of what occurs in a development" as found in experimental research of Jean Piaget.[15] Lonergan's earliest significant interpretation of Piaget's findings on operational development of humans is in his unpublished, book-length supplement to his lectures on Philosophy of Education (1959),[16] and then in subsequent thematizations of conscious operational development in his 1961 Dublin Insight lectures on "Critical Realism and the Integration of the Sciences" (1961),[17] the Gonzaga University lecture on "The Mediation of Christ in Prayer" (given in 1963),[18] in the last two essays that appeared in Collection: "Existenz and Aggiornamento" (1964), and "Dimensions of Meaning" (1965),[19]

---

[14]Bernard Lonergan, "Time And Meaning," in R. Eric O'Connor, ed., Bernard Lonergan: 3 Lectures (Montreal, Canada: Thomas More Institute, 1975), pp. 29-54.

[Hereafter abbreviated as TM with page references to the above edition.]

[15]TM, p. 42. On 'Genetic Method' see Insight, pp. 451-87; see MoT, p. 38 of the transcript by Brezovec, where Lonergan relates genetic method from Insight with his new treatment of human development.

[16]Bernard Lonergan, Philosophy of Education (Cincinnati, Ohio: Xavier College, 1959), pp. 183-95; an unpublished, book-length manuscript, supplement to the lectures; available at the Lonergan Centre, Regis College, Toronto. [Hereafter abbreviated as PE.]

[17]Cf. CRIS.

[18]Cf. MCP.

[19]Bernard Lonergan, "Existenz and Aggiornamento," and "Dimensions Of Meaning," in Fred E. Crowe, S.J., ed., Collection: Papers by Bernard

in the papers edited in A Second Collection,[20] as well as in the Latin lectures De methodo theologiae (1962), the summer Toronto institutes on "Method of Theology" (from 1962 on), and his final published version of Method in Theology (1972).[21] Together with Lonergan's earlier book-length manuscript for the lectures On the Ontological and Psychological Constitution of Christ (1956-58)[22] and his rather polemical defense of this same text against the accusations of heresy by a Roman theologian, published in Lonergan's "Christ as Subject: A Reply" (1959),[23] and with an already mentioned essay "Cog-

---

Lonergan, S.J. (London: Darton, Longman & Todd and New York: Herder & Herder, 1967), pp. 240-251 and 252-268. [Hereafter abbreviated as EA and DM , in Coll.]

[20]William F. J. Ryan, S.J. and Bernard J. Tyrell, S.J., eds., A Second Collection: Papers By Bernard Lonergan, S.J. (London: Darton, Longman & Todd and Philadelphia: The Westminster Press, 1974); see the index of names under Piaget. [Hereafter abbreviated as SC.]

[21]Bernard Lonergan, Method in Theology (New York: The Seabury Press, publ. by Herder & Herder and London: Darton, Longman and Todd, 1972), pp. 27-29 and ch. III on "Meaning." [Hereafter abbreviated as MIT.]

See also Bernard Lonergan, Philosophy of God, and Theology (Philadelphia: The Westminster Press, 1973), pp. 1-14 [hereafter abbreviated as PGT]; and Bernard Lonergan, Doctrinal Pluralism (Milwaukee: Marquette University Press, 1971 Pere Marquette Theology Lecture), pp. 13ff [hereafter abbreviated as DP].

[22]Bernard Lonergan, On the Ontological and Psychological Constitution of Christ, orig. in Latin (Rome: Gregorian University, 1956, 1957, 1958), an unpublished book-length supplement to Lonergan lectures. English translation is available from Tim Fallon, S.J. at Santa Clara University, Philosophy Department. [Hereafter abbreviated as OPC with page references to Fallon's translation.]

[23]Bernard Lonergan, "Christ As Subject: A Reply," first published in Gregorianum 40 (1959): 242-70, then republished in Coll., pp. 164-197.

nitional Structure" (1964), there is a sufficient amount of material for interpreting Lonergan's comprehensive argument from operational development.[24] I will begin my discussion of consciousness with Lonergan's early interpretation of Piaget's account of the child development. While the terms related to Lonergan's notion of mediation, and to worlds of immediacy and those mediated by meaning, are his own, in The Philosophy of Education notes he incorporates some important insights from Piaget's research.

A thesis to consider is the following: Human consciousness is immediate in the operator and mediated in the operations. At first, there is a world of immediacy into which we are thrown as infants--literally, non-talkers. It is a world which contains "only what could be seen, heard, touched, tasted, smelt, felt."[25] When one is lost in a dreamless sleep or in a coma, then one is neither conscious nor is any meaning part of one's existence.[26] Lonergan recalls the distinction between night and morning dreams developed in a thirty page essay by Ludwig Binswanger and prefaced by Michel Foucault's 130 page analysis.[27] Night dreams are influenced organically, e.g., by one's digestion, but morning dreams reveal the "existential subject," who begins to posit herself in her world during those first moments towards being awake:[28]

> The coming to consciousness in the dream of morning is patterned. The difference between the dream of

----

[Hereafter abbreviated as CSR with page references to Coll.]

[24]On human consciousness see "Cognitional Structure," in Coll., pp. 221-239, espec. pp. 222-24.

[25]PGT, p. 1.

[26]DM, in Coll., p. 252.

[27]PE, p. 199. Lonergan refers here to L. Binswanger's Traum und Existenz and to its French version Le rêve et l'existence, published by Desclée in 1954 and prefaced by a 130-page analysis by Michel Foucault. Lonergan also notes Heidegger's influence on Binswanger's development of depth psychology.

[28]Ibid.

> morning and the dream of night . .. is that there is more pattern to the dream of morning. Consciousness is a selecting, an organizing; and being awake is more organized than the dream of the morning. Patterning is essential to consciousness.[29]

Nevertheless, consciousness is not to be equated with perceiving, understanding, judging, or deliberating. Rather, consciousness denotes an infrastructure, a component within a larger compound "that easily is unnoticed until it is rounded off in combination with a manifold of further elements."[30] The difference between an unconscious and a conscious person is not one between no knowledge on the one hand and clear and distinct ideas on the other. The distinction points to the fact that in a coma or in a dreamless sleep the operations of sensing, feeling, touching, smelling, tasting, inquiring, understanding, deliberating, and deciding do not occur. When they do resume their operations as conscious, consciousness is not perception or knowledge but just "an infrastructure, a component, within knowing that in large part remains merely potential."[31]

The infant lives in a world of immediacy: it is alive and conscious, but becomes a full human person only "by mastering vast systems of symbols and adapting its muscles, nerves, cerebral cortex in order to respond to them accurately and precisely."[31] The infant develops by a self-correcting process of learning, i.e., through adaptation (adjustment, assimilation), combination and grouping of already learned schemes of operations.[32] Lonergan explains Piaget's meaning of the two poles of adaptation: assimilation

----

[29]Ibid., p. 200.

[30]Bernard Lonergan, "Religious Experience, " in Thomas A. Dunn and Jean-Marc Laporte, eds., Trinification of the World, A Festschrift for Fred Crowe (Toronto: Regis College, 1978), p. 83. [Hereafter abbreviated as RE.]

[31]Ibid., p. 83.

[32]PE, pp. 185-88; also see DM, in Coll., p. 252.

results in repeated "use of operation" already familiar to the infant, but adjustment requires the change and the modification of the already assimilated skills in order to fit the operations in a new situation.[33] The operations that are natural to the infant at birth have very low efficiency and lack economy, but they rapidly differentiate and adjust both to particular objects and to particular objects under differing conditions.

In his 1959 manuscript Philosophy of Education, Lonergan highlights the functional character in Piaget's usage of the two poles of adaptation. The notion was (1) formed by Piaget in his studies of biology, (2) then applied in psychology to child development as well as to the development of the mathematical scientist; (3) further, it distinguished between organic and psychic "development in the child, and intellectual development in the scientist discovering a new theory";[34] (4) while the three types of development are functionally analogous and structurally isomorphic, they "differ in content on each level," thus avoiding any sort of reductionism.[35] Further, Piaget's genetic structuralism differs from a number of other positions. The most important instance (from among those cited by Lonergan) for the purposes of interpreting Lonergan's account of consciousness is a difference between Piaget and Gestalt theories: "[Gestalt] is similar insofar as the scheme has a structure, a form. But the structure for Piaget is an operational structure, whereas the structure in Gestalt is within the percept."[36]

Before turning to the operational structure of consciousness, where the above points of distinction will become clearer, there remains a word to be said about the grouping of assimilated schemes of operations. As every scheme "tends to embrace the whole universe," so with a development and further grouping

----

[33]TM, p. 42.

[34]PE, pp. 185-86.

[35]Ibid. On N. Chomsky's generative grammar see Lonergan's CAM, pp. 97ff.

[36]Ibid., p. 186.

of schemes the world of immediacy is being enlarged.[37] The oral space of the infant develops prior to bodily space. The oral space is later combined with looking and grabbing. With this combination the bodily space develops.[38] An example can be given: a toddler that wanders from his mother to his father and back to his mother does not know that he is coming back--the two movements are at first two 'displacements' in space.[39] First, then, there are operations, further their combination, and finally, the two form a group of operations. With grouping of operations the toddler is able to move about in the space. Secondly, there is a grouping of groups when, e.g., manual, oral, and ocular operations are combined with manipulating the objects in nearby space. The infant becomes a master of the nursery.[40]

Mathematical group theory empowers Piaget's analysis to determine the stages in the development of the child. The child can perform only a number of operations, but there will be at each stage some points where a further grouping of operations is arrested. When a given stage is attained, there is reached a temporary equilibrium.[41] In a line of the child's development one can distinguish when a particular group of operations is mastered and when the transposition to another stage is required. "Piaget's theoretical structure gives a precise meaning to stages, and to the 'not yet attained' of stages."[42]

Once again, Lonergan highlights what is important to his own thinking in Piaget's use of the mathematical group theory:

----

[37]Ibid., p. 187; cf. CAM, pp. 54-55. Lonergan's knowledge of grouping in mathematics came long before he studied Piaget, sometime before 1953 when he was finishing his book Insight. He studied Piaget in 1959 as a preparation for his course on "Philosophy of Education" at Xavier College, in Cincinnati, Ohio; cf. the MS.

[38]Ibid.

[39]TM, p. 43; cf. CAM, p. 54.

[40]PE, p. 188.

[41]Ibid.

[42]Ibid.

> "[G]roup of operations" is used here [in Piaget] in the sense that is merely analogous to the use in mathematics. He is not talking about mathematical operations; he is talking about the operations of the child in looking, grabbing, and so on.[43]

Besides the contemporary discovery of isomorphism among the geometrical, numerical, and physical functional interrelations, Piaget's application of group theory to his psychological research disclosed an isomorphism of knowing with doing. The toddler's wandering back and forth is analogous to the adding and subtracting of spaces to one another, as is the grouping of the variables operative in human sensory-motor apparatus to the grouping of mathematical variables.

To sum up the infant's life in a world of immediacy: I have been considering the sensory-motor operations comprising assimilation and adjustment as the two poles of adaptation, schemes of operations, and grouping. There are three main points in Piaget's findings stressed by Lonergan: first, the functional, non-reductionist character of Piaget's use of group threory; secondly, the nature of the structures as operational, i.e., independent of the content-structures within percepts; and, thirdly, the primacy of operations over the structural contents in each stage of the development. Before continuing with operations on symbols, images and meanings, which is the topic of chapter III, I must return to our main concern here, the operational, self-constitutive structure of consciousness.

I began with the thesis that consciousness is immediate in the operator and mediated in the operations. The states of a coma, a dreamless sleep, the dreams of the night and morning, and waking consciousness were distinguished. A patterning was indicated in conscious operations, but consciousness

----

[43]Ibid., p. 189.

was not equated with perception, clear and distinct ideas, or knowing. I quoted Lonergan as saying that consciousness is an infra-structure, a component within the pattern of operations, largely to be unnoticed at first.

Lonergan indicates the basic pattern of conscious operations:

> seeing, hearing, touching, smelling, tasting, inquiring, imagining, understanding, conceiving, formulating, reflecting, marshalling and weighing the evidence, judging, deliberating, evaluating, deciding, speaking, writing.[44]

These operations in the basic pattern promote the infant from a world of immediacy to the world mediated by meaning. The operations are "transitive not merely in the grammatical sense [*pace* Derrida's *differance* discussed in ch. I *supra*] . . . but also in the psychological sense. . . ."[45] Consciousness is mediated by the operations of intending, but it is only through operating that one becomes aware of the intended objects. Thus, in consciousness, in seeing a color there becomes present what is seen, by hearing a sound the heard is present in hearing, by imagining there becomes present what is imagined.[46]

The operations, however, not only intend the objects and make present what is intended, but they also operate consciously, and in them the operating subject is *constituted* as present to itself as consciously operating. There figure, then, different senses of the word *presence*: (1) I can say that a chair is present in the room, (2) that you are present to me, (3) but for you to be present to me, I have to be present to myself.[47] "Just as operations by their intentionality make objects present to the

----

[44]MIT, p. 6.
[45]Ibid., p. 7.
[46]Ibid.
[47]MCP, p. 8; cf. MIT, p. 8, and CRIS, pp. 30ff.

subject, so also by consciousness they make the operating subject present to himself."[48] The intentional elements of conscious operations are the act of intending, the intended object and the intending subject as self-constituted in its presence to itself in intending.[49]

The subject as subject forms the center of immediacy, but this presence of the subject to self is not to be discerned directly, that is naively, by some act of introspection, by taking a good look or by suggesting an epistemological theory. Lonergan's analysis of consciousness on this point of one's self-presence has been subjected to some strong criticism by A. Perego, S.J. Lonergan's argument for the self-constituting character of consciousness is, however, crucial for understanding his entry into the modern and contemporary problematic with their recurrent themes of the dissolution of the subject, the death of God, and the end of history. Lonergan's 'deconstruction' of human subjectivity and of various discourses into which he entered differs from other projects of deconstructive 'archeology' or Nietzschean 'genealogy', as these appear among the tenets of the post-structuralist mind-set, by virtue of Lonergan's argument from operational development. While the post-structuralists, such as Derrida, deny a privileged place to 'presence' in the subject as subject, Lonergan argues that the center of immediacy, which the subject as conscious is, cannot be served on a silver platter for a direct, unmediated grasp, and if one tried for such a naive 'presence in-itself', there would be nothing to deal with in terms of both 'being' and the 'I'.

I noted the points that were important for Lonergan's analysis, especially the difference between the Gestalt stress on the structure of percepts and Piaget's operational and functional account of structure development. In his reply to Perego's attack, Lonergan, brings up a similar distinction "between consciousness conceived as an experience and consciousness conceived as the per-

----

[48]MIT, p. 8.
[49]MCP, p. 8.

ception of an object."[50] Lonergan's 'deconstruction' of the two positions on consciousness introduces the two options: "[I]f consciousness is conceived as an experience there is a psychological subject, while if consciousness is conceived as the perception of an object there is no psychological subject."[51]

In his lecture series "Notes on Existentialism" (1957), Lonergan presents the crux of the same argument, but now it offers the foundations for understanding contemporary relativism, pluralism of conflicting horizons and, most of all, the nonexistent or barred, displaced human subject of the post-structuralist currents of thought. Since this is a passage to which I will want to refer several times throughout the remaining chapters, and since it is a clear statement of Lonergan's overall argument here undertaken, I will quote it in full:

> The subject-as-subject is reality in the sense that we live and die, love and hate, rejoice and suffer, desire and fear, wonder and dread, inquire and doubt. It is Descartes' "cogito" transposed to concrete living. It is the subject himself in any theory or affirmation of consciousness, but as the prior (non-absence) prerequisite to any presentation, as a priori condition to any stream of consciousness (including dreams).
>
> The argument is: that the prior is not object as object or subject as object; there only remains subject as subject, and this subject as subject is both reality and discoverable through consciousness. The argument does not prove that in the subject as subject we

---

[50]A. Perego, S.J., "Una Nuova opinione sull' unità psicologica di Cristo," Divinitas 2 1958): 409-424. The cited text is in Lonergan's CSR, published in Coll., pp. 164-97.

[51]CSR, in Coll., p. 175 (italics mine).

> shall find the evidence, norms, invariants, and principles for a critique of horizons; it proves that unless we find it there, we shall not find it at all.[52]

Lonergan brings up the topic of the subject's self-presence in different contexts. In "The Mediation of Christ in Prayer" he denies that the subject's presence to herself can be the result of one's introspection or reflection.[53] For one must be present to oneself "to be able to find anything within consciousness upon which one could reflect or into which one could introspect."[54] Consciousness is neither a result of introspection, reflection, nor a matter of looking at, for

> then one would not be conscious when one was not looking at oneself and one would still be unconscious when one was, because what one would look at would be something unconscious. The looking does not change its object.[55]

Lonergan's argument proceeds negatively by offering the 'foundations' (an inverse insight) for the 'deconstruction' of simple immediacy, i.e., the fallacious claim to psychological self-presence of the subject as something perceived or looked at. The argument proceeds positively, by closer approximation to the methodological analysis of operational development. Consciousness is immediate in the operator, the subject-as-subject present to itself, and mediated in the operations by which the objects are present to the operating subject. Immediacy of the subject's self-presence differs from the presence of

----

[52]Bernard Lonergan, "Notes on Existentialism," (Boston: Lectures at Boston College, July 1957), p. 28; an unpublished mimeographed edition by Thomas More Institute, Montreal, 1957 (italics mine).
[Hereafter abbreviated as NE.]

[53]MCP, p. 8.

[54]Ibid.

[55]Ibid.

the objects: immediacy of consciousness "is constitutive of the subject as subject," and it is prior to any reflexive or introspective operations, i.e., the subject as known.[56]

Again, in "Cognitional Structure": "Objects are present by being attended to; but the subjects are present as subjects, not by being attended to, but by attending."[57] The presence of the subject as subject is not the presence of another object "dividing his attention."[58] If one tries to find oneself as subject by reaching back as if to uncover one's subjectivity, these efforts produce a mere introspecting of the different layers of subjectivity, a mere attending to the subject: "[W]hat is found is, not the subject as subject, but only the subject as object; it is the subject as subject that does the finding."[59] Hence, one's presence to self is not the same as one's knowledge of self: "To heighten one's presence to oneself, one does not introspect; one raises the level of one's activity."[59]

There exist what Lonergan calls the two pitfalls of the "psychological fallacy" and the "introspective paradox." In the latter, you want to get an experience of an insight, but if you attend to the insight, you will neglect the object of the insight, and in neglecting the object of the insight, "you will not get an insight to attend to."[60] The former, the psychological fallacy, "is substituting the concept, the definition, the explanation, the judgment for an experience."[61] The concept or a definition of an emotion, an act of understanding or an insight given in psychological literature is quite different from one's experience of emotion, understanding and reflecting. Accordingly, there figure possible fallacious readings of Insight that pose as a 'Lonerganian argument', which nevertheless, are but a mode of Aristotelian, Transcendental-Thomist, Kantian, Hege-

----

[56]Ibid., p. 9.
[57]CS, in Coll., p. 226.
[58]Ibid.
[59]Ibid.; cf. CRIS, p. 32.
[60]Ibid., p. 34.
[61]Ibid., p. 33.

lian, or other contexts of explanation by which one substitutes concepts for the conceived or the explanation for the explained:

> In the first ten chapters of Insight I try to acquaint the reader through experience of himself of what his own acts of understanding, direct and reflective, are. If a reader thinks not of his own experience, he does not bother about getting any experiences, or if he gets them he interprets what I say not by his own experience of acts of understanding but by some definition of what understanding is or some explanation. He is in the psychological fallacy.[62]

In order to know knowing--to know oneself--one does not shift an attention to the subject, but rather mediates the level of one's conscious operations. Consciousness is not "knowing knowing but merely experience of knowing"; but if knowing is just looking, then, "knowing knowing will be looking at looking"; but, Lonergan argues, that self-presence of the subject as subject is not a matter of looking at oneself, because what one would look at would still be something unconscious.[63] Once again, in order to know "what I am doing when I am knowing," I have to experience myself operating. But experience itself is not another operation, "for this experiencing is not intending but being conscious."[64] Consciousness is not another operation to be added to the operations that are being experienced: "It is that very operation which, besides being intrinsically intentional, also is intrinsically conscious."[65] Here we come back to our initial: consciousness is immediate in the operator and mediated in the operations.

The negative side--'deconstruction' through an

----

[62]Ibid., pp. 33-34.
[63]CS, in Coll., pp. 224-25; cf. MCP, p. 8.
[64]MIT, p. 8.
[65]Ibid.

inverse insight--in Lonergan's argument is best illustrated by his favorite example of knowing as 'taking a good look'. There are three perennial sources of philosophies based on 'knowing as looking': realist, materialist, and idealist. The myth of inward inspection, characteristic of the idealist view and of the 'ocular metaphor' recently deconstructed by Derrida's American counterpart, Richard Rorty, in his Philosophy and the Mirror of Nature, consists in the false analogy between cognitional events and ocular vision.[66] The analogy goes something like this: (1) Consciousness is a kind of cognitional event; (2) consciousness, then, is to be conceived on the analogy of ocular vision, which is the model for realist and materialist philosophies; (3) since consciousness cannot inspect outwardly, it must be subject to inward inspection.[67] The analogy between outward and inward inspection is the same as the one between the 'already-out-there-now-real' and the 'in-here-now-real' view of the immediate world and immediate consciousness. The idealist version of the analogy differs from the naive realist and the materialist ones in extending its argument by means of a superlook at looking. In brief, Lonergan's 'deconstruction' of these perennial oversights proceeds by an overthrow, sublation, and mediation of any philosophical starting-point based on naive, immediate attempts to grasp the notion of 'presence' as simply given--regardless of whether such a 'simple'

----

[66]Ibid. See Richard Rorty, Philosophy and the Mirror of Nature (Princeton, N.J.: Princeton University Press, 1979). Also see Thomas J. J. Altizer, et al., Deconstruction and Theology (New York: Crossroad, 1982), p. viii: "For the record we can say that deconstruction has its gallery of Gothic-faced pioneers and palladins: Nietzsche, Heidegger, Derrida, Deleuze, Foucault, Rorty." Consult also pp. 2-3 there.

On R. Rorty, Voegelin, Gadamer, and Lonergan, see Frederick Lawrence, "Language as Horizon?" in Fred Lawrence, ed., The Beginning and the Beyond: Papers from Gadamer and Voegelin Conferences. Supplementary Issue of Lonergan Workshop, Vol. 4 (Chico, California: Scholars Press, 1984), pp. 13-34.

[67]Ibid.

is conceived as 'naturally' or 'ideally' real. The very fact that Lonergan discusses perennial sources of oversights or biases in various types of materialist, realist, and idealist philosophies, rather than the classical notion of the *philosophia perennis*, is a form of 'deconstruction' of the way the question of philosophy used to be uncritically framed.

One should, however, note that there is a legitimate use of 'introspection', meaning not consciousness as such, "but the process of objectifying the contents of consciousness" through acts of inquiry, understanding, reflection, judgment, and statements about the conscious subject as subject and its operations.[68] I will have to come back to this topic vis-à-vis Lonergan's dialectical method for one's overthrow, sublation, and mediation of the 'ocular analogy' of knowing when I speak about the levels of conscious intentionality and one's self-appropriation of the operational development.

Next, I want to consider two positions in order to consolidate both Lonergan's argument and the difference between the views of consciousness as operation or object and consciousness as experience:[69]

(1) John knows his dog. (2) John knows himself.

(a) John is the subject of both (1) and (2).

(b) The object of (1) is John's dog. (b') The object of (2) is John himself.

(c) Knowing is, then, of two kinds: (1') Direct, where the object is not the subject, and (2') indirect, reflexive, where the object is the subject.

(d) "Name the reflexive knowing consciousness. Define the subject as the object of consciousness."[70]

(e) Then, consciousness is a reflexive knowing; for the knower is the known in consciousness.

(f) The subject is, then, the object of consciousness, "for whatever is known, is an object."[71]

----

[68]Ibid., p. 9.

[69]CSR, in *Coll.*, pp. 175-76; example used by me is Lonergan's.

[70]Ibid.

(g) But, a cognitive operation does not constitute its object, but merely reveals what the object is.

(h) Since consciousness was said to be knowledge of an object, it cannot have any constitutive effect upon it, but only reveal it in its proper reality.

(i) But, "if without consciousness John is simply a prime substance (such as this man or this horse), then, by consciousness John is merely revealed to himself as a prime substance."[72]

(j) Again, if without consciousness there is no other psychological presence and unity beyond the objects of his knowledge, then by consciousness John merely manifests having no psychological presence to himself as subject.

(k) Again, if without consciousness John cannot be conscious subject of physical pain, then by consciousness he manifests his incapability to suffer.

(l) It follows from (d): If without consciousness John cannot be consciously intelligent, rational, free, and responsible subject of his intelligent, rational, free, and responsible operations, <u>then, by consciousness as knowledge of an object</u>, he merely "knows himself as neither consciously intelligent, nor consciously rational, nor consciously free, nor consciously responsible."[73]

(3) Conclusion. <u>Positive</u>: The view of consciousness as perception "takes account of the fact that by consciousness the subject is known by the subject." [<u>Negative</u>:]

> <u>It overlooks the fact that consciousness is not merely cognitive but also constitutive</u>, not of what exists without consciousness, but of what is constituted by consciousness. . . . [C]onsciousness does not reveal the psychological unity that is known in the field of objects; it constitutes and reveals the basic psychological unity of the subject as subject.[74]

----

[71]Ibid., p. 176.
[72]Ibid.
[73]Ibid.

CONSCIOUSNESS AS SELF-CONSTITUTING

It is obvious from the conclusion that the definition of consciousness given in (d) through (h) is false, as shown by Lonergan in the consequent results in (i) through (l). In all the points proceeding from the erroneous analysis of consciousness, the psychological self-presence of the subject as subject is dissolved (*pace* Derrida). Not only are the subject's operations merely a kaleidoscope of incoherent acts, but what is revealed is the subject as virtually non-existent--actually barred and displaced.

The question yet pending is, how (if not directly) can the self-constitutive function of consciousness be accounted for? The alternative to the views that (1) consciousness is a matter of taking a good look, perceiving or knowing an object, (2) "only objects are known," and (3) "everything that is known, is known insofar as it is an object," is to affirm that "everything that is known, is known insofar as it is in act."[75] Thus, Lonergan is able to say that the operating subject and her operations are constituted and "known simultaneously and concomitantly with the knowledge of the objects. . . ."[76] There are, then, three *intentional elements*: (1) the operations of intending, (2) the intended object, and (3) the intending subject.[77] The object is known as "what is intended," the subject is known as he "who intends," and the operations are known both as the "intending of the subject and the . . . being intended . . . that regards the object."[78] One should not, however, confuse consciousness and the reflexive operations of consciousness. Consciousness is immediate in the subject as subject and mediated in basic operations of attending, inquiring, understanding, conceiving, weighing the evidence, judging, deliberating, and deciding. The object of conscious operations may be the things or the self. Both in the direct operations (concerning the things) and the reflexive operations (concerning the self as ope-

---

[74]Ibid., pp. 176-77 (italics mine).
[75]Ibid., p. 177.
[76]Ibid.
[77]MCP, p. 8.
[78]CSR, in *Coll.*, p. 177; see n. 14 there.

rating) the subject is present to itself not as object but as subject ("under the formal aspect of 'the experienced'").[79] This self-presence is what Lonergan calls attention to when he speaks of the self-constituting (self-mediating) function of consciousness.

In direct operations the subject is known as subject, "but in reflexive activity the subject is known _twice_, as subject by consciousness, and as object by the reflexive activity."[80] The transposition from the subject as subject to the subject as object requires a higher functional differentiation of consciousness through reflexive operations.[81] It will suffice for the moment to specify that consciousness _is_ awareness of the operations in which it is mediated, of their subject as immediately present to itself as subject, and of itself as object in heightened operations of conscious intentionality, but that _it is never knowledge of objects of operations_. Consciousness as an _infra-structure_ in cognition is the knowledge _as_ experienced, hence, in itself, it "has the indistinctness of the preconceptual. . . ."[82]

To sum up: The topic discussed in this chapter was self-mediation by consciousness. The difficulty of finding the data of consciousness, and specifying the character of 'presence' indicated by Lonergan in the subject-as-subject, is that these _are not imaginable_. Though cognitional structure is isomorphic to the general pattern of mediation, the displacement inwards of consciousness in which human development operates is not isomorphic to the previous shapes of mediation. The data of consciousness are not imaginable, hence there is no form that could enter into an isomorphic pattern of relationships:[83]

> Consciousness perceives nothing either directly or indi-

----

[79]Ibid., p. 180.
[80]Ibid., p. 178, n. 14.
[81]Ibid.
[82]Ibid., p. 181, n. 18.
[83]Ibid., p. 186.

> rectly, immediately or mediately, because what is known by consciousness is not fashioned into a "percept" like an object but is subjective and belongs to a subject not only when he is perceiving but also when he is sleeping or waking, apprehending or desiring, sensitively or intelligently operating.[84]

I have quoted supra the long paragraph from Lonergan's "Notes on Existentialism," in order to lay the ground for a discussion of the importance of his analysis of consciousness for the contemporary themes of the dissolution of the human subject, the death of God, and the end of history. Lonergan's argument for the self-constitutive function of consciousness relies primarily on operational analysis and is thus capable of furnishing both the positive and the negative foundations of the alternative approach to consciousness as perception. On the negative side, what is being deconstructed by Derrida, and others like R. Rorty, is a faulty account of consciousness (e.g., 'holding up the mirror to nature' attacked by Rorty) found in various philosophies with a naive notion of 'presence'. On the other hand, Lonergan's 'deconstruction' of the 'ocular metaphor' --the source of perennial oversights in philosophical realism, materialism, and idealism--yields a positive indication of consciousness as experience:

> Consciousness as experience is indicated [i.e., not grasped naively] when a method is described as going back and forth between experience which has been given form by understanding and conception and experience in the strict sense [i.e., consciousness]. Consciousness itself is not that method for returning nor is it the return itself but what one returns to.[85]

----

[84]OPC, p. 131.
[85]Ibid. (italics mine). On R. Rorty, note the

---

comment by F. Lawrence, op. cit., pp. 16-17: "If epistemologists have managed to misunderstand the question about knowing, this does not mean that it cannot be correctly understood and posed. More simply, if knowing is a self-correcting process--as hermeneutic philosophy supposes it shall ever be here below--this does not imply that such 'correcting' is ultimately just an arbitrary choice of a new perspective. . . . Yes, the metaphor of 'holding up the mirror to nature' may be misleading . . . but that does not warrant blatantly the Nietzschean assertion that there is 'no criterion that we have not created in the course of creating a practice, no standard of rationality that is not an appeal to such a criterion, no rigorous argumentation that is not of our own conventions.'"[The last internal reference by Lawrence is to R. Rorty, op. cit., p. 32.]

Walter J. Ong, in Orality and Literacy: The Technologizing of the Word (London and New York: Methuen, 1982) makes a poignant criticism of the textualists, as he styles Derrida's movement of deconstruction. Derrida, and others, attack the assumption of the one-to-one correspondence between the world and speech, and between the speech and writing, on which "the naive reader presumes the prior presence of an extramental referent which the word presumably captures and passes on through a kind of pipeline to the psyche. In variation on Kant's noumenon-phenomenon theme . . . Derrida excoriates this metaphysics of presence. . . . Writing breaks the pipeline model . . . . The end result for Derrida is that literature--and indeed language itself--is not at all 'representational' or 'expressive' of something outside itself. Since it does not refer to anything in a manner of a pipeline, it refers to, or means, nothing." But a 'metaphysics of presence', or logocentrism, "'corpuscular epistemology,' a one-to-one gross correspondence between concept, word and referent," lacks in Derrida's critique "any description of the detailed historical origins of what they [textualists] style logocentrism. In the absence of such an account, it would appear that the textualist critique of textuality . . . is still curiously text-bound, . . . the most text-bound of all ideologies, because it plays with the paradoxes of textuality

CONSCIOUSNESS AS SELF-CONSTITUTING

Although one cannot imagine consciousness--there is no data or form of consciousness--one can exploit the link (i.e., the data of consciousness) in which "intelligence investigates the nature of sense, imagination, intellect, will, and the soul. . . ."[86] By this link Lonergan means some "sort of thread or highway that will perhaps be of some use in relating what appear, at first sight at least, to be totally unrelated ways of understanding human life and its significance."[87]

Finally, to retrace the steps of Lonergan's argument taken thus far: A human being develops from below upwards as a self-completing animal. One moves from a world of immediacy to a far larger world, at first in the nursery and, later, in one's world mediated by meaning. But what exists prior to assimilation, adjustment, grouping, and mediation by meaning is not the object as object or the subject as object but the subject as subject. The latter is present to itself not as presented by a psychiatrist, in the pronouncements of an epistemological theory, or in an inward look of introspection, but rather as a prior "prerequisite to any presentation or introspection."[88] Unless one can find that self-presence as the source of the operational development and of history, one will not find it at all.[89] But to find that self-presence, the reader must move to the world mediated and constituted by operations on meaning.

----

alone and in historical isolation, as though the text were a closed system." [Pp. 166-69.]

[86]CSR, in Coll., p. 186.

[87]TM, p. 23.

[88]NE, p. 28.

[89]Ibid.

CHAPTER III

CONSCIOUSNESS AS MEDIATED BY MEANING

A. Introduction: Meaning

In "Dimension of Meaning" Lonergan begins with addressing the objection that meaning is just "a secondary affair" to reality, that which is meant, which is the thing that really counts,[1] and he remarks that "to all appearances, it is quite correct to say that reality comes first and meaning is quite secondary."[2] But the objection overlooks the character of human reality, "the very stuff of human living," which is not merely meant but also constituted through the operations on meanings.[3]

In this chapter, I will consider human operational development through self-mediation by meaning. In the first section (A), I will introduce the basic and derived sources, elements, and functions of meaning. Since meaning figures within a dynamic structure of human operations, I will treat in this section (1) the parts and a whole of intentional summations, (2) isomorphism of the structures of operations on meaning, (3) the problematic character of human development, (4) different dynamic patterns of human polymorphic conscious experience (the spontaneous subject), and (5) sum up the basic and derived categories of meaning. Section (B) will be an exposition of the category of meaning within the dynamic pattern of polymorphic conscious experience in the spontaneous subject. In five subsections, experiential carriers of meaning will be discussed: intersubjective, artistic, symbolic, presystematic linguistic, and (in the concluding subsection) incarnate, comprising the whole of the cultural infrastructure. The summary will focus on the import of Lonergan's analysis and prepare the transition to the concluding Chapter IV on self-

----

1 DM, in Coll., p. 252.
2 Ibid.
3 Ibid.

mediation through differentiated controls of meaning and value.

(1) Intentional summations

Besides the intentional element--the operating subject, the operations, and the intended object--there are also the intentional summations.[4] Intentional operations are summated into living, self-correcting process of learning, acquisition of new skills and ways of doing things. Intended objects are summated into situations, the situations into the environment, the environment into one's world and one's horizon. The operating subjects are summated into intersubjectivity: the community, "we," the family, "the swarm, the flock, the herd, the group."[5] "We apprehend together the common situation, act together in the common situation, communicate together about the common situation, live a common life and share a common destiny."[6]

Human consciousness is not only immediate in the operator but also in the intersubjectivity of the common "we." Human consciousness is not only mediated by the operations that make the objects present to the subject as subject, but is also mediated by the summations of operations--summations into the common living and of the objects into one's world. Human consciousness is not only self-constituting of the subject as self-present, and of the operations as a dynamic functional whole, but it also "gives rise to the 'we,' the intersubjective community . . . who live together and perform all the operations of life not singly, like so many isolated monads, but as a 'we.'"[7]

The community is "an achievement of common meaning," namely, the common field of mutually self-mediated experience, understanding, judging, deliberating, and deciding.[8] The community is the "possibility, the source, the ground of common meaning ...."[9]

----

[4] MCP, p. 9.
[5] Ibid.
[6] Ibid.
[7] Ibid.
[8] EA, in Coll., p. 244.
[9] DM, in Coll., p. 254.

But common meanings develop, they have histories,[10] they are expressed in the life of the family, polity, legal or national and international political systems, custom, commerce, industry, professions, religion, education, language, literature, art, philosophy, science, and in history as written.[11] While one is lost in a dreamless sleep or in a coma, no meaning has a part in one's life. As the infant moves from a world of immediacy to <u>the world mediated by meaning</u>, it learns through operations and grouping of operations the meaning of its immediate world in the nursery. While the immediate operations consist of adaptation and grouping of schemes of operations, there also develop the mediate operations on images, symbols, and words.[12]

The world mediated by meaning is much larger: it comprises not only the <u>present</u> and the factual, but also what is <u>absent</u>, the past and the future, the possible, the merely ideal, normative or simply fantastic:[13]

> In entering the world mediated by meaning one moves out of one's immediate surroundings towards a world revealed through the memories of other men, through the common sense of community, through the pages of literature, through the labors of scholars, through the investigations of scientists, through the experience of saints, through the mediations of philosophers and theologians.[14]

The world mediated by meaning is not a sum or the integral of the worlds of immediacy; but rather human

----

[10]EA, in <u>Coll</u>., p. 245.

[11]DM, in <u>Coll</u>., pp. 254-55; on mutual self-mediation see MCP, pp. 12-14.

[12]Cf. MIT, pp. 28-29; DM, in <u>Coll</u>., p. 253; PGT, p.1. PE, p. 189.

[13]Ibid. (all the above references).

[14]DM, in <u>Coll</u>., p. 253; cf. also MIT, p. 28; PGT, p.1.

knowing is immediate in the summations of the intentional operations and mediated by the whole of the operations on meaning. "What is meant, is not merely experienced, but also somehow understood and, commonly, also affirmed."[15] It is this larger world mediated by meaning, as understood and affirmed, that we refer to as our life world, the real world.[16]

Besides the cognitive function of meaning, i.e., "beyond the world we know about," there is the world we constitute through the operations on meaning. The humanly-made, artificial world is our engagement in the acts of meaning, when we transform nature, plan cities and industries, investigate and enter contracts, execute orders, and produce the results.[17] So it is through the effective function of meaning that we transform the world about us.

We do not only constitute the humanly-made world by transforming nature, but also by transforming the human world itself. The constitutive function of meaning plays the most obvious role in education, in "the difference between the child beginning kindergarten and the doctoral candidate writing his dissertation."[18] Just as consciousness is constitutive of the subject as subject, and "language is constituted by articulate sound and meaning," so also human institutions and cultures are constituted by meanings as the very stuff of the properly human life-world.[19]

Though common meanings "originate in single minds" and are transmitted to further generations in the education of individuals, they become common "only through successful and widespread communication."[20] The communicative function of meaning affects, besides the education of individuals, also the development of meaning in communities and in their histories.[21] The education of individuals recapitulates the longer cycle

----

[15]DM, in Coll, p. 253.
[16]Ibid.
[17]Ibid., pp. 253-54; cf. MIT, p. 77.
[18]CM, in Coll., p. 254.
[19]MIT, p. 78.
[20]EA, in Coll. p. 245; DM in Coll., p. 254.
[21]MIT, pp. 79-81.

of the education of humankind, the emergence of social institutions, and the rise of different cultures.[22]

To sum up: Human meaning is (1) embodied and carried intersubjectively, artistically, symbolically, linguistically, and incarnately in the lives and deeds of men and women;[23] (2) it is mediated in knowledge by cognitive functions of meaning: (3) it figures in human artifices and various social transformations of nature through its effective function; (4) it constitutes the properly human life-world through its constitutive function. Further, (5) what is meant is communicated to others through the intersubjective, artistic, symbolic, linguistic, and incarnate carriers of meaning; (6) meaning constitutes the common way of life and the history of the communities--their very culture; (7) inversely, with regard to the development of religion, art-forms, language, literature, science, philosophy, historical writings--their decline and renewals--"all such change is in its essence a change of meaning...." [24] (8) Besides the development from the world of immediacy to the world mediated by meaning, there emerge differentiations and controls effected by the constitutive and communicative functions of meaning. Thus, the so called low culture regards "a world mediated by meaning but it lacks controls over meaning and so easily indulges in magic and myth"; the higher culture "develops reflexive techniques that operate on the mediate operations themselves in an effort to safeguard meaning."[25] (9) Finally, in the West, the two higher cultures can be distinguished: the classicist "thinks of the controls as a universal fixed for all time; the modern thinks of the controls as themselves involved in an ongoing process."[26]

Further, the distinction between the immediate and mediate operations, inspired by Piaget and developed by Lonergan, is relevant to the above classifications. First, consciousness was said to be immediate in the

----

[22]DM, in Coll., p.254.
[23]DM, in Coll., p. 254.
[24]DM, in Coll., p. 254.
[25]MIT, p. 28.
[26]Ibid., p. 29.

self-presence of the subject as subject and mediated in the operations. Secondly, operations are immediate when their objects are present, i.e., in seeing, hearing, touching, smelling, tasting, etc., but they are mediate (with respect to what is represented or signified) when operating immediately on images, symbols, and words.[27]

Thirdly, when the operations are mediated with respect to what is present, one if freed to regard also the past, the future, the absent, the ideal, the normative, or the fantastic. One can operate not only on the environment of the nursery, but can move to the larger world of the common history, memory, and everyday culture.

Fourthly, one can operate on the mediate operations themselves in order to control or decide between meanings and values. Lonergan classifies the emergence of these reflexive operations as the cultural superstructure (the structure <u>built upon</u> the infrastructure of consciousness in which experiential carriers of meaning are functional) that historically originated in the high cultures of Greece and Europe, and now is repeated in the ontogenesis of the individuals. Finally, there is a set of isomorphisms between the developments of meaning.

<u>(2) The isomorphisms of operations</u>

In the first place, human development is marked by temporality and historicity. But

> the time of meaning is not a succession of mathematical points.... It is a now of the subject that is identical through time and of the subject that is not . . . . confined to meaning things that are present.[28]

So the isomorphisms pertain to two histories: the one

----

[27]Ibid., p. 28.

[28]TM, p. 41; on time and history see MIT, pp. 175-58.

of humankind and the other of the individual. Both are promoted by the development of meaning.

In the second place, there figure five basic types of meaning: intersubjective, symbolic, artistic, linguistic, and incarnate. These I will describe more fully later in section B of this chapter. Besides the immediate operations and the grouping of the groups, the mediate operations operate on images, symbols, and conventional signs. There emerge, however, distinct fields of operations that will not group together, i.e., limits that can be transcended only through specific transpositions in meaning and controls of meaning.[29] Reflexive techniques for the new control of meaning are developed: consciousness is differentiated from the common sense mode of operations into theoretical (displacement to systematic thinking in ancient Greece), critical (modernity in the West), transcendent (apprehension of religious meaning in various cultures) and, with respect to operations and controls themselves, methodical (contemporary third stage of meaning) exigencies of meaning. (I will define and develop these exigencies more fully later in Chapter IV of this study.) While these distinct and controlling modes of operations do not group together, there "exist fundamental terms of reference from which we can study human development generally, the development of meaning."[30] In these fundamental terms of reference, we have another case of isomorphism, between the historical differentiation of consciousness from the lower, undifferentiated to higher classical and higher modern cultures, and the individual differentiation of consciousness in the case of contemporaries; the latter accounts for the multiple horizons of meaning in contemporary culture(s).

In the third place, "when one <u>operates with respect to the operations themselves,</u> then one is studying method, or the development...."[31] One will find "the controls [of meaning] as themselves

----

[29]TM, p. 44.
[30]Ibid.
[31]Ibid., p. 45 (italics mine).

involved in an ongoing process,"[32] and the whole of human development as "the mediation of autonomy" and the emergence of the autonomous human subject.[33] There exists isomorphism between the developing historical consciousness in mutual self-mediation of the community, arts, literature, sciences, philosophy, history, theology, etc., as they work out greater autonomy of the human subject, _and_ the person's history where the individual's living "is the manifestation, the mediation of his existential decisions."[34]

This set of isomorphisms parallels the one between the different types of mediation, and it neither posits a bridge between the human subject and the world, nor a universal (i.e., extrinsic to the operations of the concrete subjects) concept of history. The character of the isomorphisms, in Lonergan's sense, is given by the concrete group of operations: first, in mediation in its general form and, secondly, in further complications of the initial theorem.

A factor is said to be immediate in the source and mediated in the outcome. Mediation can be either a mutually functional whole, a self-mediation, or a mutual self-mediation. Self-mediation is not a sum of mutual mediations, for the group of functional wholes will not integrate to produce _development_ of life. The limitations found in the stage of mutual mediation are transcended through the differentiation of the original theorem: self-mediation is a functional whole with the consequences that change the whole. Hence, the category of development requires genetic method in order to complement the statistical and classical methods.

Further, _displacement inwards_ of consciousness is isomorphic with, but different from, mediation in general and from mutual mediation. It is isomorphic because in its general form it is immediate in _x_ and mediated in _y_. It is different because it has

----

[32]MIT, p. 29.
[33]MCP, pp. 9-12.
[34]Ibid., p. 12.

consequences for the whole that change the whole. Consciousness is a case of self-mediation. Conscious self-presence is immediate in the subject as subject and mediated in the intentional operations and their summations. To indicate what consciousness is, one does not introspect. Consciousness is that prior displacement inwards, which is the prerequisite to any further presencing of interiority; consciousness is not the method but what one return to while operating methodically.

To indicate what consciousness is, one describes one's conscious operations, which can be either immediate (when the objects are present in the basic operations), or mediate (when operating on images, symbols, and words). Consciousness is not only self-constituting of its own self-presence, but also of its <u>historicity</u>; for one can consider the future and the past, the absent and the ideal, the normative and the imaginary. <u>Consciousness is immediate in the mediate operations and mediated in its historicity.</u>

Meanings have cognitive, effective, constitutive, and communicative functions. Besides a world of immediacy, there are the worlds mediated, made, constituted, and communicated by meanings. But not all mediate operations integrate in groups. There are limits to what common sense can apprehend, and to what it will accept as its criteria of meaningful life. The limits, however, can be transcended through further differentiations of consciousness.

The notions of limit, group, operator, integrator, differentiae, transcendental function, and isomorphism (as we have seen in Chapter I) are taken from mathematics. Nevertheless, the stages and the realms of development are effected not by mathematics but by operations on the side of concrete subjects. It is not mathematics that is the source of development, but concrete mathematicians are. Similarly, human history as written is not the source of historical consciousness, rather this source is concrete subjects in the myriads of common sense, literature, scholarship, science, philosophy, and theology. While for very good reasons reality comes before meaning, it is the subject who is the originating source of meaning and value, through which the reality is mediated, constituted, effected, and communicated.

So far I have considered the first of the three isomorphic questions about knowing: "What am I doing when I am knowing?"[35] This is the question in cognitional theory, and it is concerned with "an accurate account of what occurs when you are coming to know."[36] Neither the isomorphism discussed above, nor Lonergan's argument from operational development, result from the problem of the bridge between the knower and the known as raised by Descartes and Kant.

Kant's question is the second one in Lonergan's way of proceeding through inverse insight ('deconstruction'); without the proper prior analysis of the first question any answer is possible. The second question is stated emphatically in one of Lonergan's answers during a discussion:

> Why is performing this set of operations something relevant to knowing an independent reality? Why are the immanent criteria in your operations--the requirement to attend, to be intelligent, to be reasonable--what on earth have they to do with my ability to know something that is totally different from myself? That's the epistemological problem.[37]

Lonergan's argument rests on questions of the first order: questions about performing this set of operations when one is using common sense, when one is operating as an empirical scientist or a mathematician, writing history, or performing the tragedy of King Lear. Questions of the second order--the epistemological ones--are subject to 'deconstruction", sublation, and mediation in self-appropriation of operational development.

----

[35]PGT, p. 39 (see Chapter I supra).
[36]Ibid., p. 40.
[37]Ibid., pp. 39-40 (italics mine).

The third question is metaphysical: "what do you know when you do it?....What is the basic heuristic structure of everything that you are going to know?"[38] Lonergan's notion of isomorphism has its base in the first order questioning: it is the isomorphism among the basic and derived groups of operations and, further, among the different types of mediation. The basic heuristic structure of being comprises the integral of classical, statistical, and genetic anticipations of intelligibility. Nevertheless, Lonergan's argument for the isomorphism of the operational (knowing) and integral heuristic (known) structures of being hinges upon the need for one's self-appropriation of operational development. According to Lamb:

> For Lonergan it is by adverting to this conscious quality of all experiencing that he can erect the foundations of his method. There is an immediacy of the subject to himself in all conscious activity; it is so immediate that calling attention to it often seems strange.[39]

It is only in the process of development that the "subject becomes aware of himself and his distinction from his world."[40] To overlook the import of human development is to fall into the pitfalls of introspective paradox and psychological fallacy, namely, to manage a misconceived cognitional account of the subject-object split that an epistemology in vain tries to bridge, justify, or dissolve (and with this attempt at dissolution also

----

[38]PGT, pp. 39-40.

[39]Matthew L. Lamb, History, Method and Theology: A Dialectical Comparison of Wilhelm Dilthey's Critique of Historical Reason and Bernard Lonergan's Meta-Methodology (Missoula, Montana: Scholars Press, 1978), p. 257. Lamb's work was originally written as a doctoral dissertation under Johann B. Metz at State University Of Münster, West Germany.

[40]MIT, p. 29.

displace the subject and his life-worlds).[41] Lonergan suggests that we change the priority of the order of initial questioning with cognitional theory first and then deal with the second and third order questions, concerning epistemology and metaphysics, through 'deconstruction' of their oversights and biases. (This second and third order questioning is the focus of Chapter IV *infra*).

(3) The problem of human development

The problem of human development and of one's self appropriation of that development is twofold: (1) it lies in the basic fact of the *polymorphic* human consciousness--in its biological, aesthetic, dramatic, intellectual, moral, and religious *patterns of experience*;[42] and (2) there are different levels of conscious self-presence of the subject as subject--empirical, intelligent, rational, and deliberative.[43] The polymorphic character of human consciousness is protean; it varies according to patterns of experience, while these experiential patterns figure as specific sequences of sensations, images, memories, meanings, etc. [Figure 2.]

Different *carriers of meaning* are operative: intersubjective, artistic, symbolic, linguistic, and incarnate. These carriers exemplify the different patterning of conscious experience. But it is only through the development of language from its ordinary and literary forms to technical embodiments of meaning that one is able to enter critically into the intellectual pattern of experience. Through the intellectual pattern of experience, conscious intentionality is promoted by wonder and questions from empirical self-presence to intelligent, rational, and existential (deliberative, responsible) self-presence. The levels of conscious self-presence

---

[41]Cf. Frederick Lawrence, op. cit., pp. 16-17; (see n. 68 to Chapter II *supra*).

[42]Cf. *Insight*, pp. 181-89, 385-87, 530-49 (see the references in notes 56-58 below, and the subsection 4 of this chapter, on different classifications of the patterns of experience).

[43]CRIS, pp. 31-32.

refer to the interrelated sets of operations which constitute empirical, intellectual, rational, and responsible wholes. The whole of the four levels comprises a dynamic cognitional and existential structure of human living. [Figure 3.]

LEVEL OF CONSCIOUS SELF-PRESENCE	PATTERNS OF EXPERIENCE	SUBJECT
EMPIRICAL SELF-PRESENCE	biological, aesthetic, dramatic,intellectual, moral (practical), religious	SPONTANEOUS

Figure 2. Polymorphic character of human consciousness

One moves from a world of immediacy to the world mediated by meaning: first, in the purely experiential patterns of meaning, and later to the world mediated and constituted by language; further, from the world of the ordinary and literary languages to the world of theory. Finally, only in the critical self-appropriation of the polymorphic character of conscious intentionality, through heightening of one's experience in understanding, in judging that understanding of experience, and in deliberating about meaning and value of living and operating, can one return methodically to the intersubjective base of the common meaning, of literature, and of the ongoing historical contexts of theories.

(4) The spontaneous subject and the patterns of experience

Immediacy of the infant's consciousness is not static but a formally dynamic structure that admits differentiations of the basic operations and to subsequent higher integration of those differentiations. Consciousness is self-constituting of the formally dynamic recurrent pattern of experiencing, understanding, judging, and deliberating (see Fig. 3). This structure is common to all human, historical subjects.[44] People, however, are not just knowers.[45]

As Lamb remarks:

LEVELS OF CONSCIOUS INTENTIONALITY	FORMS OF BASIC OPERATIONS	CARRIERS OF MEANING
EMPIRICAL	<u>Patterns of Experience</u> biological aesthetic dramatic intellectual moral (practical) religious	intersubjective artistic symbolic linguistic: --ordinary --literary --technical
INTELLIGENT	UNDERSTANDING	DISCOURSE
RATIONAL	JUDGMENT	SPHERES OF BEING + CONTROLS OF MEANING
RESPONSIBLE	DELIBERATION	

<u>Figure 3. A whole and the parts of a basic dynamic cognitional structure</u>

> Attention to conscious experiencing means that Lonergan is well aware of the limitations of knowing as knowing. Human consciousness is not some computer-like apparatus... the human subject is capable of many varied patterns of conscious experiencing.[46]

----

[44]Lamb, <u>loc. cit</u>.
[45]Cf. CRIS, p. 35.
[46]Lamb, <u>o.p. cit</u>., p. 260.

And in Lonergan's own words:

> You do not simply have a structure of experiencing, inquiring, imagining, understanding, thinking, reflecting, grasping the unconditioned and judging.... Besides purely cognitional activities there are affective acts, loving and hating, desiring and fearing, enjoying and enduring, deliberating, choosing, carrying out one's decisions....[47]

On the level of spontaneous self-presence all these operations form a single, undifferentiated, and interdependent whole. The spontaneous subject does not simply know. Her sensing is mediated immediately by affectivity; understanding and judging are directed immediately to deciding; and what she thinks about or seeks to understand and judge is connected with things of her immediate praxis.[48] The spontaneous subject is concerned with particular, concrete reality, with what is useful and immediately practical. She lives in the concrete. It is the whole human being that operates, not just a knower.[49]

The spontaneous subject does not study persons as such, but knows concrete persons in a variety of concrete situations. His learning does not follow any theory but depends on the intersubjective, artistic, symbolic and incarnate carriers of meaning. He speaks the language studied by Wittgenstein in ordinary language analysis.

The spontaneous subject belongs to her own family, a tribe, town, regional culture, country: "The rest of the world is made up of foreigners."[50] She knows

----

[47]Cf. CRIS, p. 35.
[48]Ibid.
[49]Ibid., p. 40.
[50]Ibid., p. 39.

truth, virtue, values, reality insofar as concrete practicality is concerned. The spontaneous subject never adverts to the principle of contradiction, and when she does, then such an expression of the principle is embodied in the affect-laden image, a symbol. "A symbol is . . . . an image which pours over into affectivity, that conveys a meaning and mediates an apprehension of value."[51]

The operations of the spontaneous subject can be studied theoretically. They can be taken to be an exemplification of the particular stage in the ontogenesis of the individual. One can distinguish the structure and dynamism of consciousness, the spontaneous view of the world, the mode of its learning, the types of symbolic and linguistic expression in which meaning and value are expressed and communicated. The spontaneous subject is, however, also the subject in any primitive, low culture. He represents the particular cultural stage in apprehension of the world, of meaning and value. Similarly, "a man lying on the beach and enjoying the warmth of the sun" is an example of a spontaneous subject pertaining to any possible cultural or ontogenetical stage of development.

The method of investigation of the 'subjective field' on the level of empirical self-presence brings us back to the notion of patterns of experience.[52] As sensation is never isolated from its bodily basis, bodily movements, and from the dynamic context of other events, so "both the sensation and the bodily movements are subject to an organizing control."[53] Besides the "systematic links" among the bodily basis, sense, and the skeleto-muscular movements in space and time, consciousness also streams in many different patterns. This conscious stream involves not merely "the temporal succession of different contents" and "a factor variously named conation, interest, attention, purpose," but also comprises variable direction of the stream itself.[54]

----

[51]Ibid., p. 40.
[52]Cf. <u>Insight</u>, pp. 181 ff.
[53]Ibid., p. 182.
[54]Ibid., cf. NE, p.3.

Lonergan's often cited example of the variable (polymorphic, protean) pattern of conscious intentionality is Thales and the milkmaid: "Thales was so intent upon the stars that he did not see the well into which he tumbled. The milkmaid was so indifferent to the stars that she could not overlook the well."[55] It was the intellectual pattern of experience that made Thales attentive to the well, and it was the milkmaid's practical concern that made her disinterested in the pursuit of knowing for its own sake.

Lonergan distinguished in his various writings the six or seven patterns of experience: (1) both the dreams of night and of morning,[56] (2) biological, (3) aesthetic, (4) dramatic, (5) intellectual, (6) practical or moral,[57] and (7) religious (worshipful or mystical) patterns.[58] I have already mentioned in Chapter II Lonergan's interest in L. Binswanger's analysis (and M. Foucault's extended commentary) of the dreams of night and of morning. The aesthetic, dramatic, practical, religious, and intellectual patterns will be discussed later, together with different carriers of meaning. Now, the most primitive and basic among these experiential patterns in which human meanings are embodied and communicated is the biological pattern of experience. I will briefly illustrate what the biological pattern of experience is.

The operations in the biological pattern of experience "converge upon terminal activities of intussusception or reproduction or, when negative in scope, self-preservation."[59] On the scale of values, the vital, physiological need of air, water, nutrition, sleep, shelter, and sex predominates. The extroversion of these basic, vital functions and the "confrontational element of consciousness" are characteristic of the conation, emotion, striving, and purposiveness in the biological pattern of experience.[60] Here the basic

----

[55] Insight, p. 182.
[56] Cf. NE, p. 3.
[57] Only in MIT, p. 29, 286; and in Lamb, op. cit., pp. 265-66.
[58] Ibid.
[59] Insight, p. 183.

operations of adaptation, grouping, and mediation are not so much concerned with the "immanent aspects of living, but with its external opportunities."[61]

SOURCES OF MEANING

OPERATIONAL DEVELOPMENT — adaptation: [assimilation-adjustment] grouping self-mediation: [consciousness, meaning, controls of meaning] — CATEGORIAL REALIZATIONS

FUNCTIONS/
COGNITIVE-COMMUNICATIVE-EFFECTIVE-CONSTITUTIVE

ELEMENTS/

Consciousness/
EMPIRICAL-INTELLIGENT-RATIONAL----DELIBERATIVE

ACTS/ Potential-Formal-------Full-------Performative

TERMS/Undifferen-
tiated----Conceived----Judged-----Valued

Carriers of meaning/ intersubjective--linguistic:---Universe of discourse /worlds and spheres of being/
artistic, symbolic — ordinary, literary technical

Controls and Exigencies of Meaning — theoretical critical transcendental methodical

Figure 4. Sources, elements, and functions of meaning

----

[60] Ibid., p. 184.
[61] Ibid.

Before going to our main theme in this chapter concerning the various carriers of meaning, I will outline Lonergan's terminology of the basic and derived relationships--the sources, elements, and functions--of meaning.

(5) Sources, elements, and functions of meaning

Meaning is embodied and carried in human intersubjectivity both in different experiential patterns of conscious intentionality and on all four levels of the subject's self-presence: "in art, in symbols, in language, and in the lives and deeds of persons."[62] The sources of meaning are the "dynamism of intentional consciousness," and the categorial realizations reached through intentional operations.[63] These sources pertain to the subject as conscious in dreams, in different patterns of experience, and on all four levels of conscious intentionality.

The sources of meaning are, then, the operations (and their categorial realizations) of the subject as present to itself in these different patterns and on the four levels of consciousness. [Figure 4.] Since the sources are affected by the operational development, and since one's self-knowledge is attained only in one's self-appropriation of that development, the varieties of the experiential patterns and of the levels of consciousness will yield different elements of meaning.

The elements divide according to their sources into (a) acts or operations and (b) the terms or the categorial realizations of meaning. To the four levels of conscious intentionality correspond the four acts of meaning: (1) empirical self-presence/ potential acts, (2) intelligent self-presence/ formal acts, (3) rational self-presence/ full acts, and (4) responsible self-presence/ active or performative acts.[64] There are also instrumental acts of meaning, which are the thematizations for others of the potential, formal, full, and performative acts of meaning of the subject.

----

[62]MIT, p. 57.
[63]Ibid., p. 73.
[64]Ibid., p. 74.

The terms of meaning, or "what is meant," may be either undifferentiated, merely conceived, determinate in judgements, or settled in one's attitudes and deliberate choices.[65]

To sum up: "[T]he all inclusive term of meaning is being, for apart from being there is nothing. Inversely, the core of all acts of meaning is the intention of meaning."[66] The set of basic, related, and recurrent operations of conscious intentionality has as its all inclusive term the integral anticipation of intelligible reality--the integral heuristic structure--namely, the protean notion of being. This heuristic notion of reality is isomorphic with the core of all operations on meaning. The self-correcting process of learning is isomorphic with the core of all operations on meaning. The self-correcting process of learning is isomorphic with emergent probability in a world process,[67] and the integral heuristic structure of the operations is isomorphic with the integral mediated pattern of the all inclusive term of meaning [Figure 5.]

The isomorphic character of the sources and terms of the operations is engendered through the four cognitive, effective, constitutive, and communicative functions of meaning.[68] The general theorem of the functional relations says that a function of x will be immediate in the source and mediated in the outcome. The relation of the functions, sources, and elements of meaning is the one of mediation: the originating source of meaning and value is the subject as operating on all four levels of conscious self-presence. The terminal categorial realizations of meaning and value are the experienced, understood, judged, and deliberately chosen. Meaning is immediate in the sets of recurrent, dynamic structures of human interiority and mediated in the interlocking sequences of classical, statistical, genetic, and dialectical intelligibility. Mediation of human intelligence by intelligibility exhibits, thus, a

----

[65]Ibid.

[66]Insight, p. 358 (italics mine).

[67]Cf. Ibid., pp. 448ff.; also pp. 115-128; on history see pp. 209-211.

[68]For definition of the four functions of meaning see Part A. of Chapter III; consult also Fig. 4.

basic ontology of meaning.

The ontological aspect, the reality, pertains to meaning and value, and to the sources, elements, and functions of meaning, no matter what their content or carrier.[69] As cognitive, what is meant is real; as constitutive, meaning constitutes the properly human world, one's horizon, one's operational ability to assimilate, and one's knowledge and acceptance of values. As effective, meaning persuades others and promotes one's operations for the sake of transforming nature. As communicative, meaning carries to the hearer some aspects of the cognitive, constitutive and effective meaning of the speaker.[70]

POLYMORPHIC/ PROTEAN: HEURISTIC NOTIONS	HEURISTIC STRUCTURES	INTEGRAL HEURISTIC STRUCTURE
The core of all ACTS of meaning	intelligibility	the all inclusive TERM of meaning
anticipation and methods of investigation	classical, statistical genetic, dialectical	being

Figure 5. The all inclusive term and the core of all acts of meaning

Meaning is not opposed to reality, and while cognitive and constitutive functions of meaning differentiate the domains of fact and value, and of natural and human sciences, meaning is not mere subjective meaning.[71] The dimensions of meaning that mediate our conscious living "do not belong to some shadowy world that really does not count ... 'intentional' is not opposed to 'real'; it is opposed to 'natural'."[72]

----

[69]MIT, p. 356; cf. TM, p. 38.
[70]Ibid.
[71]TM, p. 38.
[72]Ibid., p. 39.

While human living is not constituted merely by meaning and value (for there is the reality of our bodies with their physiology and the biological pattern of experience), the ontology of meaning pertains not only to different types and carriers of meaning but also to diverse stages of meaning, to differentiations of consciousness, and to the plurality of cultural traditions.[73] Without meaning human living is incomplete. Without meaning, there would be no common life, no symbols, no art-forms, no languages or literatures, no religion, no science and history, no philosophy and theology, no family and society, no politics and economy, and no culture.[74] Without meaning, one could still be defined as rational animal, "but it would always be the rational animal that had not got to the point yet where it had learned any language or been able to signify anything."[75] The basic ontology of meaning specifies one's conscious being in the world as always apprehended through self-mediation, and one's discourses about 'being' as something never simply present, given or mirrored, but rather mediated by different experiential carriers of meaning.

B. Meaning Within the Polymorphic Pattern of Experience

Meaning is embodied in intersubjectivity, in art-forms, in symbols, in conventional signs, and in the common way of life.[76] There are, then, the intersubjective, artistic, symbolic, linguistic, and incarnate carriers of meaning. I will begin with Lonergan's thematization of intersubjectivity.

(1) Intersubjective carriers of meaning

Prior to the 'we' found in the love between an 'I' and a 'thou', there is operative the intersubjective 'we', which precedes the distinction of subjects and

---

[73]MIT, p. 356.
[74]TM, p. 38.
[75]Ibid.
[76]MIT, p. 57.

"survives its oblivion."[77] While there exists the spontaneous subject, who raises the arm to "ward off a blow" against an attack, there also operates inter-subjective spontaneity, when one reaches out to help another from falling down.[78] In "Time and Meaning," Lonergan offers his personal example of the latter:

> [L]eading up to the Borghese Gardens in Rome, where I usually go for my favorite walk, there's a ramp; coming down the ramp was a small child running ahead of its mother. He started to trip and tumbled; I was a good twenty feet away but spontaneously I moved forward as if to pick up the child. There's an intersubjectivity, there is a sense in which we're all members of one another before we think about it.[79]

Although the conscious operations of perception, of feeling and movement, are present, one adverts to them not prior to their occurrence but concomitantly with them. That prior 'we' is vital and functional.[80]

Lonergan refers to Max Scheler, who was the principal investigator of intersubjective meaning.[81] Scheler calls both the community of feeling, and one's fellow-feeling, intentional responses. For example, while parents can feel their sorrow for their dead child, a third party might be moved in fellow-feeling by the sorrow of the parents.[82] An example of community of feeling is liturgical worship: all are concerned with God, but some might be moved to prayer by the devotion of others.[83]

----

[77]Ibid.
[78]Ibid.
[79]TM, p. 31.
[80]MIT, p.57.
[81]Cf. TM, p. 31; Lonergan refers to Max Scheler's Forms of Sympathy and to Manfred Frings' Max Scheler (Pittsburg and Louvain, 1965), pp. 56-66; cf. see MIT, p. 57.
[82]MIT, p. 58.

On the other hand, psychic contagion and emotional identification are not intentional but vital responses. An emotion may be contagious without one's adverting to the object of the emotion. The laugh and the sorrow of others is contagious without one's knowing the object of the sorrow and grief.[84] "Such contagion seems to be the mechanism of mass-excitement in panics, revolutions, revolts, demonstrations, strikes...."[85] During these situations the vital responses take over one's intelligent and responsible operations. Psychic contagion can be orchestrated and exploited by politicians, corporation executives, or religious leaders.[86]

In emotional identification, one's personal identity is either yet underdeveloped or it is subsumed to vital unity. There is the emotional identification between mother and child, or "of a little girl's play with her doll," when she identifies with her mother and projects her mother's identity into the doll.[87] But personal differentiation of one's identity can be subsumed under emotional identification in the state of hypnosis, or in sexual intercourse, or the mystical experience "with a pantheist implication."[88] In the ancient mysteries, this emotional vital unity is discernible in different identifications of primitive mentality, or in the rituals during which the shaman in the state of ecstasy proclaimed himself to be divine.[89]

Lonergan illustrates the intersubjective carriers of meaning by his example of the <u>phenomenology of a smile</u>.[90] In the first place, a smile does not consist only of the movements of lips, facial muscles, head, eyes, but it also embodies a meaning.[91] "Because there is a meaning we do not walk about the streets smiling

----

[83]Ibid.
[84]Ibid.
[85]Ibid.
[86]Ibid.
[87]Ibid.
[88]Ibid., p. 59.
[89]Ibid., pp. 58 and 59.
[90]First appears in the text of TM, p. 31; cf. MIT, p. 59.
[91]Ibid. (both references <u>supra</u>).

at everyone we meet, we would be misunderstood if we did."[92]

In the second place, a smile is highly perceptible as a meaningful "patterned set of variable movements, and it is recognized as a whole."[93] Perceiving is not merely a function of the impressions on the sense; it selects those impressions that are subject to a meaningful pattern. "We have to learn to walk, to talk, to swim; we do not have to learn to smile ... we do not have to be taught the meaning as a smile..."[94]

In the third place, the meaning of a smile is everyone's own discovery which we make on our own; and that meaning is invariant cross-culturally.[95] In the fourth place, a smile is unexplainable outside of meaning or by other meanings. A smile is not univocal as language aspires to be; it is not true as opposed to false (though a simulation of a smile is possible); it is not a meaning of propositions; and it is not objective in the same sense language is.[96] "The meaning of a smile is global; it expresses what one person means to another; it has the meaning of a fact...."[97]

Finally, the smile is not about any object; rather it <u>betrays</u> the subject in her transparency or hiddenness. The smile is "a meaning with its significance in the context of antecedent and subsequent meanings."[98] While the smile reveals the incarnate subject, it also "antedates all subsequent analysis that speaks of body and soul, or of sign and signified."[99] In its equivocal, multifarious function, the smile carries the meaning of Derrida's 'play of difference', or his deconstruction of the differential structure of the signifiers as envisioned in de Saussure's linguistic structuralism. Nevertheless, the incarnate sub-

----

[92]TM, p. 31.
[93]MIT, p. 59.
[94]TM, p. 31.
[95]MIT, p. 60.
[96]Ibid.
[97]Ibid.
[98]Ibid.
[99]Ibid., p.61.

ject, who engenders an initial communication through smiling, has not yet entered either an oral or a written context of meaning. The precocious, i.e., pre-linguistic, _différence_ of the human smile grounds the very possibility that Derrida might be read by _others_, intelligently understood within the intersubjective community, or merely smiled at with an approval or bewilderment.

Besides the smile, other types of intersubjective meaning precede linguistic meaning and can be studied in many different forms of _body language_: in movement or pause, in tone or pitch, in volume or silence of the voice, in feeling hidden, revealed, betrayed or "depicted by actors on stage."[100] The source of intersubjective meaning is the spontaneous subject operating as present to itself and to others empirically. That is the reason why Lonergan stresses that a 'we' of intersubjectivity antecedes any other 'we' constituted by mutual self-mediation.

The acts and terms of the intersubjective carriers of meaning are undifferentiated and merely potential. "Such is the meaning of the smile that acts simply as an intersubjective determinant....[101] The four functions of meaning also remain undifferentiated. Intersubjective meaning effects, communicates, and constitutes the common human world; but it antedates and makes possible all the worlds mediated and constituted by meaning. Intersubjective meaning is being communicated in a world of immediacy prior to being apprehended intelligently, rationally, and responsibly; in its ontological aspect, however, what is revealed about the source of meaning is real. Any further development of the common meaning is affected by the process of communication.

> On the elementary level this process had been described as arising between the self and the others when, on the basis of already existing intersubjectivity, the self makes a gesture, the other

----

[100]Ibid.
[101]Ibid., p. 74.

> makes an interpretative response, and the self discovers in the response the effective meaning of his gesture.[102]

To conclude: a common meaning and a common language arise on that spontaneous basis "from intersubjectivity, through gesture and interpretation .... "[103] Prior to art, symbols, science, morality, and religion, there are the tasks set by the everyday form of life. This pattern of experience, in which the spontaneous subject shares a common meaning, is called by Lonergan _dramatic_.[104]

In the _dramatic pattern of experience_, the dynamic and recurrent operations of conscious intentionality focus on concrete living with style and forms of life varying in different cultures and groups. It is within this dramatic pattern of experience that the common meaning and the formation of community are the primary concern.[105] The non-intentional emotive states and intentional emotive responses[106] create the intersubjective matrix of common experience and of shared common meaning, on which common understanding, common judgment, and common commitment are built up in mutual self-mediation:[107]

> Community is not just an aggregate of individuals within a frontier, for that overlooks its formal constituent, which is common meaning. . . . Such common meaning is doubly constitutive. In each individual it is constitutive of the individual as a member of the community. In the group of individuals it is constitutive of the

----

[102]Ibid., p. 357; reference is made by Lonergan to Gibson Winter's _Elements for Social Ethics_ (New York: MacMillan, 1966, pb. 1968), pp. 99ff.

[103]Ibid.

[104]_Insight_, pp. 187-89.

[105]Lamb, _op. cit._, p. 432.

[106]Cf. MIT, p. 30ff.

[107]Cf. MIT, p. 79.

community.[108]

(2) Artistic carriers of meaning

Artistic meaning is carried in the aesthetic pattern of experience, which is marked by a greater liberation from the biological purposiveness--a liberation in a "spontaneous, self-justifying joy."[109] "Beyond the biological account-books of purposeful pleasure and pain," there is a joy of experience for the sake of experience in a world of children's play, in youthful games, "in the exhilaration of sun-lit morning air," or in the rhythm of melody.[110] Freedom of the aesthetic pattern is twofold: it liberates spontaneity from its biological concerns and from sensitivity, and it liberates intelligence from the constraints of proofs, verifications, and factualness.[111]

Lonergan borrows Susanne Langer's definition of art as "the objectification of a purely experiential pattern."[112] The meaning of experiential pattern is elemental; the functions and the terms of meaning are not formally and fully differentiated.[113] The world of the artistic subject is a transformed world; it can be taken as a mere illusion but also as heightening and revealing what truly is real. Not only does a purely experiential pattern transform one's world, but also transforms the subject who "has been liberated from being a replaceable part adjusted to a ready-made world... [and who] has become just himself: emergent, ecstatic, originating freedom."[114]

David Tracy describes the character and meaning of

---

[108]Ibid., pp. 356 and 357.
[109]Insight, p. 184.
[110]Ibid., cf. MIT, p. 29.
[111]MIT, p. 185.
[112]First mentioned in PE, pp. 199ff; cf. MIT, pp. 61ff. Reference is made by Lonergan to Susanne Langer's Feeling and Form: A Theory of Art (New York: Charles Scribner's Sons, 1953), no page reference is given.
[113]MIT, p. 63.
[114]Ibid.

the artistic world: "Meaning here refers not to 'messages' however lofty but to reality, to being, to that human and more-than-human 'issues' of things which artists as the 'antennae of the race'... allow the rest of us to hear."[115] The work of art does not merely bring forth the freedom from practicality, sensitivity, and the intellectual concerns; the art constitutes the virtual universe and reveals the world of imagination, hopes, sorrows, dreams, and subconscious life of the human subject. Art discloses human possibilities and breaks through the biases and distortions of common sense practicality or intelligence.[116] In that revelation of human possibilities, the function of art is political and therapeutic.

Artistic carriers of meaning lie within the immediate self-presence of the artist and are embodied in the mediating expression of art itself. But the process of objectifying these elemental meanings requires detachment and separation from the artist's experience. While the smile reveals the whole range of intersubjective feelings prior to any reflection, "artistic composition recollects emotion in tranquility."[117] The work of an artist consists of insights into elemental meaning, and the expression and elaboration of those insights result in "an idealization of the original experiential pattern."[118] Nevertheless, the work of art is not one's biography: "it is not telling one's tale to the psychiatrist."[119] Art presents what is important at the moment: one's concern, a truer experience, a possible novel world. Art invites one to appreciate by participation (and not by clarification through concepts), to try to

----

[115]David Tracy, The Achievement of Bernard Lonergan (New York: Herder & Herder, 1970), p. 215.

[116]Cf. Garrett Barden, "The Intention of Truth in Mythic Consciousness," in Philip McShane, ed., Language, Truth and Meaning (Notre Dame, Indiana: University of Notre Dame Press, 1972), p. 28; this is an edition of the selected papers from the first Lonergan International Symposium held in 1970 in Florida.

[117]MIT, p. 63.

[118]Ibid., p. 64.

[119]Ibid.

experience the art work for oneself, to free oneself from practicality for the sake of creative possibilities.

Lonergan, together with S. Langer, defines art as "the objectification of a purely experiential pattern." First, there is a pattern, and it can be either abstract, as in a sonata form, or concrete, as in colors and their relationships, or in shapes and volumes. But the pattern is experiential only when realized concretely: when the music is performed, when the pattern of the indentation on a record is actually reproduced in sound, when the colors, volumes, shapes, and movements are perceived.[120]

Secondly, the artist is concerned with the experiential pattern. Waking consciousness is more patterned than the dreams of the morning. The pattern in speech or in a tune is more perceptible than street noises.[121] Verses help us to remember, decorations catch our attention to the surfaces of the drapes, the rhythm, and melody enable us to repeat a song. Our experience is patterned, "because to be conscious of anything involves a patterning of what is perceived, and a pattern of the feelings that flow out of and are connected with the perceiving."[122]

Thirdly, in art we speak of a purely experiential pattern. A pure pattern excludes alien patterns that tend to instrumentalize experience.[123] An example of the pattern that instrumentalizes experience is the reaction of a driver to a red light or stop sign. The driver's senses are instrumentalized to connect the lights or signs with the movement of the car.[124] A purely experiential pattern is not the one of a scientist whose experience is patterned by conceptualization, nor one "reshaped by a psychological or epistemological theory."[125] Those are all different ways in which experience may be instrumentalized. In a

---

[120]Ibid.
[121]PE, p. 200.
[122]Ibid.; cf. MIT.
[123]Ibid., p. 201.
[124]MIT, p. 61 and PE, p. 201.
[125]PE, p. 201.

similar manner, art under the guidance of "didacticism, moralism, or social realism," such as "the Russian art that attempts to inculcate communist doctrine," is not the objectification of a purely experiential pattern.[126]

The operator in a purely experiential pattern is one's openness to awe, adventure, greatness, the uncanny, the daring. The pure pattern of experience is not curtailed by any theory: "[I]t has its proper rhythm, just as breathing has...."[127] But the pattern of the rhythm may complexify into a larger organic form. The whole thus created exhibits an "inevitability of form," e.g., in the variety and complexity of a symphony.[128]

Fourthly, the elemental meaning of a purely experiential pattern does not fully differentiate between the acts and the terms of meaning. The elemental meaning exhibits "the ontic of which Heidegger speaks";[129] it transforms both one's world and the subject operating in that experiential pattern. But the art is the <u>objectification</u> of the elemental meaning. This objectification of the artistic pattern is effected by the functions of meaning. The process of objectification is analogous to the process of moving from the <u>inner word</u> to its unfolding in insight and definition. As the scientist's wonder becomes detached in her desire to know, so also the artist works in a certain "psychic distance" and idealization of the initial experience. "Art is the abstraction of a form where the form becomes idealized by the abstraction. But the form is not conceptual."[130]

Finally, the abstract form of the relations between colors, shapes, volumes, rhythm, and the melody "is <u>isomorphic</u> with the idealized pattern of experience."[131] The idealized pattern is isomorphic with the dynamic image of a purely experiential pattern

----

[126]Ibid., p. 202.
[127]Ibid., p. 203.
[128]Ibid.
[129]Ibid.
[130]Ibid., p. 204.
[131]Ibid., p. 207.

of conscious intentionality: it is the isomorphism between "the pattern in the work and the pattern of the free experience."[132]

(3) Symbolic carriers of meaning

I have been describing the self-constituting, spontaneous subject in a purely experiential pattern of experience. What characterizes the work of art is the objectification of one's prior freedom from the biological concerns, instrumental practicality, and theoretical pursuits. That prior freedom is the prerequisite for the freedom on one's deliberate choice, and it is this prior freedom which is being explored in the artistic synthesis relevant to concrete living.[133] Lonergan enhances the need for freeing these artistic potentials within one's spontaneity:

> That exploration is extremely important for our age, when philosophers for at least two centuries through doctrines on politics, economic, education, and through ever further doctrines, have been trying to remake man, and have done not a little to make human life unlivable. And to make it livable again, the great task is the recreation of the liberty of the subject, the recognition of the freedom of consciousness.[134]

Again, Lonergan's analysis of human consciousness as a self-constituting presence of the subject as subject to itself is a key to our understanding of his thematization of freedom. Normally, we tend to think of the freedom of the will, "as something that happens within consciousness."[135] But one's deliberate freedom is already a control over the patterned flow of consciousness; nevertheless, that flow itself is inherently free and undetermined by ecology, the

----

[132]Ibid.
[133]Ibid.
[134]Cf. NE, p. 24.
[135]PE,p. 220.

objects, or by "the new biological demands of the subject.... In the freedom of consciousness itself, art is a fundamental element."[136] Briefly, Lonergan's account of human consciousness as self-constituting points to the source of novelty and creativity as founded in the subject's operational development from the freedom of consciousness to that of a deliberate self-appropriation of a prior freedom of experience.

The free flow of consciousness in the aesthetic pattern of experience is symbolic. Art is symbolic: its expression in symbols is post-biological, pre-scientific, and pre-philosophic.[137] The symbols attain their term and value, yet without defining meanings; they reach the depths of the human psyche, yet in reaching the depth, the symbols transcend it.[138] Art expresses human wonder "in its elemental sweep," free both from the constraints of sense and of intellectual systematization. "For the animals, safely sheathed in biological routines, are not questions to themselves. But man's artistry testifies to his freedom."[139]

A symbol is an affect-laden image of a real or illusionary object that evokes or is evoked by a feeling.[140] Now feelings can be related to objects, to one another or to their subject.[141] One's feelings are related to objects when focused on the objects of desire, fear, enjoyment, or sorrow. The feelings are related to one another when one hopes for some good in the future, enjoys the good of the present, or fears the evil that is absent. Feelings are related to one another in sequences and groups: either in their common relationships or despite the conflict they express. Thus one is not only able to love, enjoy, or be gentle and compassionate, but one can also hope against hope, mix love with hatred or sadness with joy.[142] Feelings are related to their subjects as the carriers, embodiments, actuation, and orientation of one's

----

[136]Ibid.
[137]Ibid.
[138]*Insight*, p. 185.
[139]Ibid.
[140]Ibid.
[141]MIT, p. 64.
[142]Ibid.

conscious life.

The affective responses exhibit different stages in affective development. Symbols themselves are expressive of these different stages, of their progress and aberration, and can be evoked or evoke certain affects within the particular stage. The difference between the aesthetic and the symbolic is manifest in the affectively undifferentiated orientation and interchangeability of some instances of the latter. The symbolic is the genus comprising the species of both the aesthetic and non-aesthetic. The work of art objectifies the aesthetic pattern, but symbols admit and reflect affective development, differentiation, increase or reduction in intensity, combination and higher integration of their signifying values. Whereas art is the objectification of the purely aesthetic experience, the symbolic, including its non-aesthetic aspects, can enter the compounds and conglomerations of "undifferentiated or only slightly differentiated symbols."[143]

Lonergan gives the example of St. George and the Dragon, who represent "at once all the values of ascensional symbolism and all the disvalues of the opposite."[144] There are affective development and aberration, and these call for a "transvaluation and transformation of all values."[145] The Dragon may become Jonah's Whale and St. George, a drowning man swallowed by the Whale, vomited without any harm after three days on a nearby shore. It is apparent how the new development in affects have transvalued the symbolism of St. George and the Dragon. But there are symbols that do not accept transformation and transvaluation; they express a developmental block.[146] Instrumentalization of experience and the influence of rationalism did not eliminate the symbolic and the affect-laden from human life, but rather they led to their devaluation and vulgarization. "Hera and Artemis

----

[143]Ibid., pp. 64-65.

[144]Ibid., p. 65.

[145]Ibid., p. 66; "transvaluation of values" supra signifies Lonergan's transposition of Nietzsche's phrase.

[146]Ibid.

and Aphrodite were replaced by the pin-up-girl, and Paradise Lost by South Pacific."[147]

The significance of the symbolic and artistic in human life is their power to reveal the affect-laden depth of human relationships to the world, to one's notion of space and one's journey in it, and to one's time reference. There is, then, in art and symbol "a possible interpretative significance,"[148] as there is in the development of the child, or in the development of such notions as space, time, and human journey in philosophy and in natural science. As the mediation of immediacy by meaning can effect one's methodical self-appropriation of the cognitional process, so also one can discover, identify, and accept one's "submerged feelings in psychotherapy."[149] The interpretation of the elemental symbolic meaning will, however, be mediated by the linguistic carriers of meaning. The fact that there are many interpretative contexts of art and symbol "only reflects the many ways in which human beings can develop and suffer deviation."[150] The symbols themselves do not follow the rules of logic but rather of image and feeling.[151]

The symbolic is not concerned with logical classes, univocity, or the principle of contradiction, but with many multiple meanings and their variations: "It is overdetermined, just as in dreams."[152] All sorts of reasons and many images enter the process of communication in order to express the same point of the symbolic. The symbols do not move on one single track

---

[147]PE, p. 210.

[148]Ibid., p. 211.

[149]MIT, p. 77. Lonergan's phrase quoted supra gave impetus to Robert Doran's doctoral work on Jung, Ricoeur, and Lonergan, published as Subject and Psyche: Ricoeur, Jung, and the Search for Foundations (Washington, D.C.: The University Press of America, 1979).

[150]Ibid., p. 67. On different interpretative systems of dreams, symbols, and art--Freud, Jung, Adler, Ricoeur, Eliade, Frye--see MIT, pp. 67-69 and references there.

[151]Ibid., p. 66.

[152]PE, p. 208.

(they are not a system of pure signifying differences), but they bring together many different dimensions of one's life.

> The symbol, then, has the power of recognizing and expressing what logical discourse abhors [and what Derrida highlights]: the existence of internal tensions, incompatibilities, conflicts, struggles, destructions.[153]

Long before logic and dialectic were conceived, the symbol was able to embrace the concrete dynamism of contradictions in a way that these methodical techniques cannot.[154]

There are cognitive, constitutive, effective, and communicative functions affecting the symbolic carriers of meaning: "[I]t is through symbols that mind and body, mind and heart, heart and body communicate."[155] The cognitive function of symbolic meaning is elemental in the same way as in a smile or in a purely experiential, aesthetic pattern of experience in art. The constitutive function of symbolic meaning indicates the healthy or aberrant development of one's psyche, of one's imagination and perception of the world. Its effective function is being expressed in the symbolic "stance to nature" and other people. The communicative function of symbolic meaning "has its proper context in the process of internal communication in which it occurs...."; i.e., the context of "images and feelings, memories and tendencies...."[156] Though the acts and terms of the symbolic meaning remain undifferentiated, it is to those contexts within the human psyche that any interpretation and thematization must turn.

4. Linguistic carriers of meaning: pre-systematic language

Lonergan has broadened the too narrow view of the

----

[153]MIT, p. 66.
[154]Ibid.
[155]Ibid., p. 67
[156]Ibid.

word 'meaning' by extending it to non-linguistic patterns of experience. He was thus able to mean what appears to be the deconstructive aspect of Derrida's différence within the play of signifiers. So far, the three types of elemental meaning were distinguished--the intersubjective, artistic, and symbolic. In a parallel manner, besides the biological pattern of experience, we discussed the dramatic and aesthetic patterns, in which the spontaneous, waking subject operates. These patterns demonstrate the polymorphic, protean fact of human consciousness (the prior prerequisite even of Derrida's project of deconstruction):

> The mind is polymorphic; it has to master its own manifold before it can determine what utterance is, or what is uttered, or what is the relation between the two; and when it does so, it finds its own complexity at the root of antithetical solutions.[157]

In potential acts of meaning, the meaning and the meant are undifferentiated. The elemental meaning is spontaneous and polyvalent, and it cannot be communicated otherwise but within the intersubjective contexts of its occurrence. But in the development of language, there emerges the greatest, most novel liberation of meaning.

While the conventional signs may be combined, multiplied, differentiated into ordinary and literary languages, specialized in technical or theoretical languages, they may also be used "reflexively in the analysis and control of meaning itself."[158] Elemental meaning, however, is restricted to spontaneous subjects and their intersubjective expressions. For even the aesthetic conventions are constrained by colors, shapes, volumes, sounds, and movements of a purely experiential pattern.[159] Elemental meaning is, of course, subject to interpretation in therapy, to

----

157 Insight, p. 386.
158 MIT, p. 70.
159 Ibid.

phenomenological analysis, or to art criticism--all of which heighten the concealed cognitive, constitutive, effective, and communicative functions of the intersubjective, artistic, and symbolic carriers of meaning.

Linguistic signs are the instrumental acts of meaning, i.e., expressions that "externalize and exhibit for interpretation by others the potential, formal, full, constitutive, or effective acts of meaning of the subject."[160] But language is not a mere addition to the other acts of meaning. There is the isomorphism between the sensible expression of language and the basic pattern of the intentional operations.[161] Linguistic expression is the "sensible and proportionate substrate" of interior acts of conceiving, judging, and deciding, in a similar manner as sensible data are supposed by inquiry, images by insight, and relevant evidence by judgment.[162] The operational development--adaptation, grouping, mediation--of human intelligence grounds the fact of isomorphism between the structure of language, the basic pattern of operations, the acts and terms of meaning, and the functions of the inner word and their outer, instrumental expressions in written or spoken language. For example, in studying operational development in Aquinas, Lonergan was not satisfied with simple 'archaeological digs' into Aquinas' written discourse, but was in fact 'deconstructing' that discourse, and the commentaries thereof, for the sake of retrieving Aquinas' subjectivity not as something to be merely looked at and then mirrored in the manuals, but as intelligently operating. In Verbum, Lonergan comments on his methodology of literary criticism:

> Now to understand what Aquinas meant and to understand as Aquinas understood, are one and the same thing; for acts of meaning are inner words, and inner words proceed intelligibly from acts of understanding. Further, the acts

----

[160]Ibid., pp. 75 and 86.
[161]Ibid., p. 86.
[162]Ibid.

> of understanding in turn result from empirical data illuminated by agent intellect; and the relevant data for the meaning of Aquinas are the written words of Aquinas.... To understand the text, to understand the meaning of the text, to understand as Aquinas understood, are but a series of different specifications of the same act.... Still, if method is essential for the development of understanding, it is no less true that method is a mere superstition when the aim of understanding is excluded.... [T]he temptation of the manual writer is to yield to the conceptualist illusion; to think that to interpret Aquinas he has merely to quote and then argue; to forget that there does exist an initial and enormous problem of developing one's understanding....[163]

Again, in Insight:

> To penetrate to the mind of a mediaeval thinker is to go beyond the words and phrases.... It is to discover for oneself that the intellect of Aquinas, more rapidly on some points, more slowly on others, reached a position of dynamic equilibrium without ever ceasing to drive towards fuller and more nuanced synthesis, without ever halting complacently in some finished mental edifice....[164]

It is meaning that differentiates spoken words from

----

[163]Bernard Lonergan, Verbum: Word and Idea in Aquinas (Notre Dame, Indiana: University of Notre Dame Press, 1967), pp. 215-217 (italics mine). [Hereafter abbreviated as VWIA.]

[164]Insight, pp. 747-48; see also MIT, p. 30.

other noises, and the written words from mere marks on a piece of paper. Both coughing and speaking are produced in the respiratory tract, but only the latter carries the inner word of the speaker.[165]

The difficulty with operational development of the child does not consist merely in the difficulty of learning words to speak and write, but also in learning the universe of new meanings. "So it is that conscious intentionality develops and is moulded by its mother tongue."[166] Lonergan, referring again to Piaget's research, says: "the child would like to have its own grammar, much more logical in his mind than the one learned."[167] The learning of the mother tongue involves the child in the socialization of its mind: by imitation of the adults and in the symbolic play of its own.

What precedes the more mature development of language is symbolic play, in which the child lives in a world of pretense. Lonergan gives another example from the daily walk he used to take in the Borghese Gardens in Rome. He describes a group of children playing cops and robbers. Some of them possess very expensive toys but others just wooden sticks. The children with the sticks have just as good a time as the ones with expensive toys: "it is all make-believe."[168] During the time of symbolic play, the child is also learning by imitation of others. Imitation aids the adaptation by adjustment, whereas play promotes the adaptation by developing more complex assimilative powers. Lonergan sums up Piaget's discoveries on this point:

> As the group of operations is developed, there occurs a concomitant development...of the world and...of the self-conscious subject.... [At first] there is a minimum objectivity and subjecti-

----

[165] VWIA, pp. 1-2.
[166] MIT, p. 71.
[167] PE, p. 189.
[168] Ibid.

> vity...[then] assimilation and adjustment become ever more differentiated.[169]

Objectivity is the outcome of the grouping of groups of operations, and not simply of "the play of perception and associations."[170] The different sensory-motor schemes multiply, combine, differentiate, and group into the child's world, a horizon. "The horizon corresponds to the group of operations mastered."[171] While Lonergan's operational analysis of consciousness differs from the views of consciousness as perception, also his notion of horizon is different from the meaning given to it by Kant or Husserl.[172] A

----

[169]Ibid., p. 191.

[170]Ibid.; the citation supra is from Piaget's series of Studies in Genetic Epistemology; edited by W.E. Beth, W. Mays and J. Piaget, Etudes d'épistemologie génétique Vols. I-III (Paris: Presses Universitaire de France, 1957).

[171]Ibid. On horizon-analysis, consult the work of D. Tracy, op. cit.., and Lonergan's NE, CRIS, and index under "horizon" in MIT.

[172]Cf. I. Kant's Logic, trans. by Robert Hartman and Wolfgang Schwartz (Indianapolis and New York: Bobbs-Merrill, 1974), especially pp. 44-45: "The horizon thus concerns judgment on, and determination of, what man can know, what he needs to know, and what he should know." Cf. also Edmund Husserl, Ideas: General Introduction to Pure Phenomenology, trans. by W.R. Boyce Gibson (London: Collier-MacMillan, 1962), sc. 24: the horizon is the "co-present margin: of perception, "a dimly apprehended depth of fringe of indeterminate reality."

In Lonergan, horizon corresponds to (1) one's concern; (2) the group of operations mastered; (3) the range of things the subject is conscious of; (4) the six contemporary horizons: common sense, art, science, scholarship, philosophy, and religion. On dialectic within horizon-analysis, see Mark Morelli's digest of his doctoral dissertation in an essay "Horizonal Diplomacy," in Matthew L. Lamb, ed., Creativity And Method: Essays in Honor of Bernard Lonergan, S.J. (Milwaukee, Wisconsin: Marquette

horizon, in Lonergan's sense, is not to be taken merely as a categorial possibility of what can be known, nor does it result from a perceptual Gestalt. One's horizon is determined and developed through basic operations and the group of operations that come under one's own control. We can speak of an infant's horizon limited to the nursery, of an artistic horizon, of a dramatic horizon concerned with practicality, of different philosophic horizons, of cultural horizons, or of the horizon oriented to self-transcendence in religious faith.

Prior to the operational control of one's horizon, there figures the stream of the self-constituting, conscious self-presence of the subject as subject, which grounds the possibility of both development and of the emergence of novel horizons.[173] One's horizon is the limit set by the type of operations one has mastered; it is the boundary between the known operations and those one knows not how to command. The existence of one's horizon is indicated by the stages in one's development; thus "a horizon in which the old appears as a part."[174]

Essential to the notion of horizon is its ontological dimension. Speaking about Piaget's account of the differentiation of objectivity and subjectivity, Lonergan gives his evaluation:

> I do not think Piaget is to be criticized because he talks as though the real world is something that is constructed. I do not think that "construction" is a word that makes one an idealist or a subjectivist. It does for people who think that knowing is taking a good look at what is already out there now.... Piaget has to be completed by adding a fuller appreciation of the subject, of

----

University Press, 1981), pp. 459-74.

[173]NE, p. 28.

[174]Ibid., p. 26.

what has meaning to the subject.[175]

As consciousness and the self-present human subject cannot be reached through one's perception, or introspection, so also the world of being, because it is mediated and constituted by meaning, may not be known by taking a good look; for being is nothing to be grasped by searching for its reality as some essence already-out-there-now. Self-conscious or metaphysical 'presence' is never an immediate percept, a clear and distinct principle, a simply given utterance, or a mark on the paper. The 'presence' here in question is what cannot be absent if self-consciousness, perception, principles, and being are to be rendered as meaningful. Again, Lonergan specifies his position on the source and core of meaning:

> The world mediated by meaning is for the naive realist just an abstraction; for the idealist it is the only world we know intelligently and rationally, and it is not real but ideal; for the critical realist it is the world we know intelligently and rationally, and it is not ideal but real.[176]

In order to illustrate that moment when language enters the human operational development, Lonergan draws upon Helen Keller's discovery "that the successive touches made on her hand by her teacher conveyed names of objects."[177] In the moment of her discovery she expressed her profound excitement and desire to learn at once more names of objects. Lonergan compares Keller's discovery of naming with prizing the ability to name in ancient civilizations.[178]

In naming, conscious intentionality becomes more focused in ordering one's presence in the world about.

----

[175]PE, p. 193.
[176]EA, in Coll., p. 244.
[177]MIT, p. 70.
[178]Ibid.

There is a difference between an impersonal existence in the dreams of the night, in one's growing self-presence at daybreak, and in focusing that self-presence in writing, listening and speaking.[179]

Language enables us not merely to name the things that are present to us, but also to talk about them in their absence. Language moulds the intentional operations and "structures the world about the subject."[180] The basic pattern of intentional operations is reciprocal, isomorphic; so languages have spatial adverbs and adjectives, different tenses of the verbs, modes of varying intentions, active and passive voices that shift the relations between the subject and object.

> Grammar almost gives us Aristotle's categories of substance, quantity, quality, relation, action, passion place, time, posture, habit, while Artistotle's logic and theory of science are deeply rooted in the grammatical function of predication."[181]

As one moves from a world of immediacy to the world mediated by linguistic meaning, there emerges an <u>exponential advance</u> of the novel language development.[182] Vocal signs are fixed by visual signifiers; words are organized in dictionaries which analyze grammar, control inflections and combinations of meanings; literary criticism evaluates composition; logic stresses clarity, coherence, and rigor; hermeneutics examines the relations between the acts and terms of expressed meanings; and philosophy effects the differentiation between the world of immediacy and the subsequent controls of meaning and value in the worlds mediated and constituted by meaning.[183]

----

[179]Ibid.
[180]Ibid., p. 71.
[181]Ibid.
[182]Ibid., p. 92.
[183]Ibid., pp. 28-9; also pp. 92ff. On genesis of language see pp. 86ff.

Finally, language can reflexively mediate, objectify, and examine the exponential advance of language development itself.

Ordinary language pertains to the day-to-day level of culture and to different common manners of living. It is spoken at home and at school, in industry and in the market, in the media and during a cocktail party. Ordinary language is transient and elliptical; it forms the basis of common sense communication. It is principally concerned with the present moment and is satisfied with simple phrases.[184] Common sense language is descriptive; it relates the concrete situations and things to subjects and to their desires, fears, hopes, and sorrows. Common sense can be shared by a group or a culture: "when it is just personal, it is thought odd; when it pertains to the common sense of a different group, it is considered strange."[185]

Literary language stands between ordinary and technical languages. It is not transient or elliptical, nor is it strictly logical or merely symbolic. Literary language is permanent; it is not just concerned with the moment for its own sake. It is a written language, a style to be appreciated, apprehended and remembered in the absence of the mutual self-presence of people.[186] It is also a fuller language than are the elliptical and transient expressions of common sense. Literary language uses similes, metaphors, synecdoches, and other symbolic devices. Grammarians and logicians named these symbolic expression "figures of speech," for they did not "quite understand why people live and talk in the apparently irrational way they do."[187] The fact is, that though words do demonstrate logical structure, symbolic consciousness operates on the affect-laden images, to which the non-literary criteria of a logical mind (e.g., logocentrism attacked by Derrida) do not apply.[188]

----

[184]Ibid., pp. 71-2.
[185]Ibid., p. 72. On common sense, see Insight, chs. VI and VII.
[186]Ibid.
[187]PE, p. 209.

(5) Incarnate meaning: cultural infrastructure Discussion and summary

The point of this subsection is to discuss the themes that were treated on the preceding pages, and to prepare the transition to the next chapter on the differentiation of consciousness in cultural development of meaning. First, the notion of incarnate meaning will be related to Lonergan's account of cultural infrastructure. Secondly, the question of human development will be put in the context of implicit definition and of mediation, as applied to consciousness and to transcendental notions. Thirdly, the problem of cognitional and moral self-transcendence will be briefly indicated as a tension between one's limitations and one's thrust towards authentic subjectivity, which in turn grounds authentic objectivity. This discussion will lay the ground for the last chapter, in which cognitional and moral self-transcendence will be treated from a perspective of the historical development of the cultural stages of meaning.

Incarnate meaning combines in mutual self-mediation the intersubjective, artistic, symbolic, and linguistic carriers of meaning:

> It is the meaning of a person, of his way of life, of his words, or of his deeds. It may be his meaning for just another person, or for a small group, or for a whole national, or social, or cultural, or religious tradition.[189]

Incarnate denotes what Lonergan means by 'cultural', 'cultural immediacy', or 'cultural infrastructure'--the whole of meaning within the polymorphic infrastructure of experiential patterns of consciousness. As consciousness was said to be an infrastructure within the larger whole of a dynamic structure of

----

[188]MIT, pp. 72-3.
[189]Ibid., p. 73.

cognition, so cultural infrastructure incarnates elemental and pre-systematic linguistic carriers of meaning, on which the higher theoretical, critical, transcendental, and methodical controls of meaning operate within the larger whole of mediation, namely within cultural superstructure.

Cultural, over and above the common way of life and the social, designates "the meaning we find in our present way of life, the value we place upon it, or, again, the things we find meaningless, stupid, wicked, horrid, atrocious, disastrous.[190] Cultural immediacy refers to the meaning in dreams before any interpretation, the meaning of a purely experiential pattern of art before being dissected by the critics, or the meaning carried in many variable intersubjective, symbolic, and everyday ways of life.[191]

The cultural is distinct from the social. The social expresses a manner of life people observe in the family; their manners in the society and its classes, in the state with its laws, in economy and technology, and in the churches.[192] Cultural infrastructure stands to social order "as the soul to body... "[193] Cultural infrastructure simply pertains to "a set of meanings and values informing a common way of life, and there are as many cultures as there are distinct sets of meanings and values."[194] In all the different cultures, there are operative the elemental and linguistic meanings, for they are the spontaneous "substance of every culture."[195] Cultural infrastructure comprises meanings immanent in

----

[190]Bernard Lonergan, "Belief: Today's Issue," in SC, p. 91. [Hereafter abbreviated as BI.]

[191]BI, in SC, p. 91.

[192]Bernard Lonergan, "The Absence of God in Modern Culture," in SC, p. 102. [Hereafter abbreviated as GMC.]

[193]Ibid.

[194]MIT, p. 301. Cf. other definitions of culture, e.g., Coll., pp. 232-33; NE, pp. 30-31; MIT, p. xi; SC, pp. 102-103.

[195]GMC, in SC, p. 102.

undifferentiated consciousness, i.e., those meanings prior to any thematization, critique, or control.

Again, cultural values are distinct from both the vital and the social ones. _Vital_ values are oriented to the particular good of the individual and communal living. Vital values, such as strength, health, or vigor, are manifest in the purposiveness of the biological pattern of experience. _Social_ values are vital to the community, and so technology, politics, and economy pursue the good of order for the sake of the common way of life. It is the dramatic pattern of experience that is concerned with the practicality of common living.[196] _Cultural_ values and meanings mediate and constitute human living and operating: "It is the function of culture to discover, express, validate, criticize, correct, develop, [and] improve such meaning and value."[197]

Because cultural meaning and value inform our common way of life, it is possible to classify cultures according to the manner in which meaning and value are apprehended, communicated, and controlled.[198] The crucial issue here hinges upon the _Meno paradox_ already mentioned in Chapter I _supra_, i.e., the question of human development: "How is it that mortal man can develop what he would not know unless God has revealed it?"[199]

Lonergan's answer to the question of development was treated at first in its most general way. The notion of mediation enabled us to define any factor _x_ implicitly--by using the theorem that the function of _x_ is immediate in its source and mediated in the outcome. In living organisms, the general notion of mediation was complicated by a further notion of self-mediation. Living development is a form of self-constitution by a novel displacement upwards in the physical parts, speciation, and ecological

----

[196]Cf. MIT, pp. 28-31.
[197]Ibid., p. 32.
[198]Cf. GMC, in SC, pp. 102-103.
[199]MIT, pp. 302 ff.; cf. Plato's _Meno_, Stephanus n. 80d.

interdependence. Besides classical and statistical laws, genetic method was introduced, and development was studied in conjunction with the general notion of mediation: development was said to be immediate in the operator and mediated in the integrator.

Human conscious development proceeds by displacement inwards; consciousness is a dynamic, materially and formally self-constituting functional whole. First, there is development from infancy to adulthood. A non-talker moves from a world of immediacy to the world mediated and constituted by meaning and value. Growing up comprises many operations of adaptation, grouping, and mediation. One's spontaneity comes to be freed from sensitivity, and one's apprehension of the world is mediated by different carriers of meaning. Consciousness is not only self-constitutive of its own self-presence, but also of the novel emergence of the cultural insfrastructure--incarnate meaning.

The dynamism of conscious intending is self-constitutive, immediately of the presence of the subject as subject to itself, mediately of the basic, recurrent operations in the dynamic pattern of conscious intentionality. Shortly, human consciousness mediates itself as self-constitutive of novelty and, by its intentional operations, of the all-inclusive term of anticipated intelligibility, i.e., being. As consciousness is defined implicitly through the set of operations of conscious intentionality, so its all-inclusive term is apprehended, at first implicitly, through the integral set of heuristic structures--the classical, statistical, genetic, and integral heuristic structures of being. Apart from psychological presence, there is no human subject, and apart from intelligent anticipation of intelligibility by this same subject, it is meaningless to speak of being. Though neither of the two (consciousness and anticipated intelligibility) is to be grasped as an immediately given, both are indicated as the prior prerequisite, the non-absence, of human development.

Lonergan's response to Meno's query and to "Plato's point in asking how the inquirer recognizes truth when he reaches what, as an inquirer, he did not know,"[200] is the invitation to one's self-appropriation of the mediating operations by heightening one's conscious intentionality. In his original unpublished Preface to Insight, Lonergan says:

> So it is that the present work is a program rather than an argument. It begins not by assuring promises but by pressuring readers. It advances not by deducing conclusions from the truths of a religious faith or from the principles of a philosophy but by issuing to readers an invitation, each more precise and more detailed, to apprehend, to appropriate, to envisage in all its consequences, the inner focus of their own intelligence and reasonableness.[201]

What corresponds to the implicit ideal of the term sought-for in an inquiry is the implicit notion of the ideal as operative in the transcendental notion of meaning.

In the transcendental notion of meaning, there is a combination of ignorance and knowledge: if we already knew what we were looking for, we would not have to bother seeking; but in seeking an unknown, we already appeal to that ideal implicitly.[202] And our appeal to that ideal is conscious, intelligent, rational, deliberate, and methodical. It is an ideal expressive in the notional imperatives: be attentive, be intelligent, be reasonable, be responsible, be in love, acknowledge your historicity! The aim of an inquiry, at first defined only implicitly, can become conceptually explicit in many different ways throughout

----

[200]Insight, p. xxii.

[201]Bernard Lonergan, "The Original Preface of Insight,", previously unpublished working draft (June 1949 to September 1953); Method: Journal of Lonergan Studies, Vol. 3. No. 1 (March 1985), p. 3. [Hereafter abbreviated as OPI.]

[202]UB, pp. 2-23.

the course of human history. Such a pursuit of an ideal is named by Lonergan "an ongoing discovery of mind,"[203] i.e., an ongoing appropriation of the intellectual pattern of experience. Thus the above _transcendental notions_ of conscious intentionality are:

> comprehensive in connotation, unrestricted in denotation, invariant over cultural change.... [They are] the radical intending that moves us from ignorance to knowledge. They are _a priori_ because they go beyond what we know to seek what we do not know yet.[204]

They are _unrestricted_, because they are never fully and explicitly conceptualized; they are _comprehensive_, because they intend the all-inclusive term of which the answers are only a part.

Operational development is made possible because of the self-constituting dynamism of the transcendental notions, and that dynamism is not a product of cultural development, but is a prior prerequisite to any development of meaning. Operational development is possible because human consciousness is also self-constitutive of the subject's thrust towards _self-transcendence_. The transcendental notions, which function as notional imperatives, promote the subject from the level of empirical self-presence to higher levels of conscious intentionality: intelligent, rational, and responsible self-presence.

The transcendental notions provide the _criteria_ for self-transcendence. These criteria are operative in one's attentiveness, intelligence, reflectivity, and deliberation. The criteria are satisfied in the self-transcendence of the human subject: in a judgment of fact, they are cognitive criteria, and in a judgment of value, they are the criteria of moral self-transcendence.[205] While the _promotion_ to self-

----

[203]MIT, pp. 305-18.

[204]Ibid., p. 11-12. [Cf. Lonergan's response to Plato's _Meno_, 80d.]

transcendence emerges with the relevant questions for intelligence, reflection, and deliberation, the criteria are satisfied when a meaning is understood, when what really is so or is not so is affirmed in judgment, and when one deliberately chooses between what is or is not truly good and worthwhile.[206]

The criteria for cognitive and moral self-transcendence are always in the concrete. For the affirmation of the real and true in judgment consists in the fulfillment of the pertinent conditions. Hence, human judgments of fact are virtually unconditioned. There are always possible further relevant questions which promote human enquiry to an ever fuller account of reality. Moral self-transcendence, likewise, is not in the abstract, for "only the concrete is good."[207] There are always possible further open-ended questions for deliberation: Is it good? Is it worthwhile? Why ought I to do it? Our moral self-transcendence is, then, a limited achievement, because "the transcendental notion of the good so invites, presses, harries us, that we could rest only in an encounter with a goodness completely beyond its powers of criticism."[208]

The promotion and criteria for cognitive and moral self-transcendence, according to Lonergan (and contrary to Kant's division between the speculative and practical reason, and to Max Weber's split between fact and value), differ in content but not in their pattern.[209] In both the judgment of fact and the judgment of value, there is the same distinction between the criteria and meaning. The criteria originate in the self-transcending dynamism of conscious intentionality; meaning and value are the terms independent of the intending subject. They are

----

[205]Ibid., pp. 36-37. [Cf. Lonergan's indirect response to the issue of the context of discovery and the context of justification in the so-called Meno paradox as treated by contemporary philosophy of science.]

[206]Ibid., pp. 35-37.

[207]Ibid., p. 36.

[208]Ibid.

[209]Ibid., p. 37.

independent cognitively when affirmed in judgment as truly so or not; they are independent morally when the intended value and meaning are deliberated about as either good and worthwhile or not good and worthwhile.

The problem of both cognitive and moral self-transcendence lies in the fact that "the being of the subject is becoming,"[210] that we are subjects "as it were, by degrees."[211] Genuine objectivity is a fruit of authentic subjectivity, and as such, it is attained not through some surrogate for objectivity but through one's development.[212] One must learn to distinguish between object and objectivity in dreams or in a world of immediacy, and in the world mediated by meaning and motivated by value. It will become apparent that in the world mediated and constituted by meaning and motivated by value, objectivity results from genuine development towards authentic subjectivity and freedom promoted by notional imperatives.

Objectivity in natural and human sciences differs only insofar as the former concerns the world mediated by meaning and the latter the properly human world, constituted by meaning and motivated by value. Both types of science, however, have the same grounding inasmuch as objectivity in science, philosophy, scholarship, and theology results from authentic subjectivity.[213]

Not only individuals but also cultures and civilizations develop towards greater authenticity, rational and moral self-transcendence. Becoming and growth of authentic objectivity in culture result from a long historical, ongoing discovery of mind, the discovery of which, in turn, mediates and enhances further development towards the rational and moral autonomy of the civilization(s). Therefore, to change the controlling meaning and value in culture is to

----

[210]EA, in Coll., p. 241. See also Bernard Lonergan, "The Subject," in SC, p. 80. [Hereafter abbreviated as Sub., in SC.]

[211]MIT, pp. 265 and 292.

[212]Ibid., p. 265.

[213]MCP, pp. 9-11.

change the reality of the shared life. To change the normative sources of meaning and value is to transpose the previous controls of meaning and value expressive of culture; it is the transposition of the very meaning of what 'culture' stands for:[214]

> For if social changes and cultural changes are, at root, changes in the meanings that are grasped and accepted, changes in the control of meaning, mark off the great epochs in human history.[215]

In the next chapter, I will return to Lonergan's argument by considering the three stages of meaning and the differentiated controls of meaning that figured in cultural mediation and constitution of human development. The issue in Lonergan's argument is the paradox and the tragedy of human being:

> Yet if man can scale the summit of his inner being, also he can fail to advert to the possibility of the ascent or, again, he can begin the climb only to lose his way.... For it is the paradox of man that what he is by nature so much less that's what he can become; and it is the tragedy of man that the truth, which portrays him as actually he is, can descent like an iron curtain to frustrate what he would and might be.[216]

Lonergan's argument is a strategic program, an invitation to one's self appropriation of the latent, creative resources for change:

> [T]here is a sense in which, I believe, it is true to say that the facts about man can be outflanked.

----

[214]Cf. DM, in Coll., pp. 255 ff.
[215]Ibid., pp. 225-56.
[216]OPI, p. 3.

> For a change in man, a development of potentialities that are no less real because, like all potentialities they are latent, not only is itself a fact but also can be a permanent source of new facts that cumulatively alter the complexion of the old.[217]

---

[217]Ibid.

CHAPTER IV

CONSCIOUSNESS AS DIFFERENTIATED THROUGH CONTROLS OF MEANING AND VALUE

A. Introduction

In "Dimensions of Meaning," Lonergan introduces his notion of the control of meaning.[1] He begins there by countering the objection against the primary importance of the mediating and constitutive function of meaning in our apprehension of 'being' about us. The progression of his thought is already familiar to the reader of the preceding chapters: it moves from a world of immediacy, where reality comes before meaning, to the world mediated and constituted by meaning and motivated by value.

Lonergan's overall argument has, then, two parts. First, he shows how what we generally refer to as real is the world mediated and effected by meaning. The properly human world, the world by which men and women transform and express the common meaning and value of their living and operating, is constituted by elemental and linguistic carriers of meaning.[2]

Secondly, it is in the field of the constitutive function of meaning that the possibilities of human freedom and responsibility are at their greatest. Lonergan thematizes the emergence of the existential subject as the highest form of self-mediation. This emergence of self-constituting human autonomy is to operational development what the differential equation is to solving the mathematical function. The subject on the level of responsible self-presence becomes the source of possible novel development, i.e., the source of its own diversifications functioning differently

----

[1] DM, in Coll., pp. 252-67.
[2] Ibid., p. 255 and Lonergan's summary there in the first paragraph.

under variable conditions. In brief, Lonergan's analysis of operational development comes closest to what might be described as the differential equation for human subjectivity: the differentiation of the transcendental functions of conscious intentionality.

Nevertheless, the equation does not guarantee one's cognitive and moral self-transcendence. In that sense, Lonergan's argument is not a deductive proof; rather it contends that, if one is not to find the source of one's development in the subject as subject, then there will not by anything else to replace it. Further, the argument proceeds by showing that being, without one's intelligent and rational self-consciousness, ceases to be anything intelligible that could enter one's horizon. It is in this measure that Lonergan distances himself from classical modern epistemology, classical natural law ethics, and traditional philosophical proofs for God's existence and opts for a thematization of intellectual, moral, and religious conversion of the subject.

An underlying aspect in Lonergan's argument is, what he calls, "the paradox-and tragedy" of human beings. The paradox consists in the character of one's self-knowledge:

> If then [one] knows himself as in fact he is, he can know no more than that he has been cast into the world to be afflicted with questions he does not answer and with aspirations he does not fulfill.[3]

The tragedy comes, when the truth about human beings as they are becomes normative for further development. Lonergan attempted to work out a programmatic method that would break through the veil of the opinions that we have about ourselves that philosophers try to suggest we should take as normative. Such a breakthrough is itself a new fact that can become a permanent source of new facts that cumulatively alter the complexion of the old facts of paradox-and-tragedy. Lonergan's argument, then, leads one to a strategic realization of

----

[3] OPI, p. 3.

one's latent sources of development; and this realization, in turn, reflexively mediates a cumulative development. Lonergan admits that his is an ambitious program; nevertheless, he finds it to be a radical response to the kairos of our time:

> In the midst of this widespread disorientation, man's problem of self-knowledge ceases to be simply the individual concern inculcated by the ancient sage. It takes on the dimensions of a social crisis. It can be read as the historical issue of the twentieth century. If in that balance human intelligence and reasonableness, human responsibility and freedom, are to prevail, then they must be summoned from the dim and confused realm of latent factors and they must burst forth in the full power of self-awareness and self-possession.[4]

Next, Lonergan generalizes his argument on the process of historical self-appropriation of autonomy in the development of the cultural stages: "It is there [in control of meaning and value] that individuals become alienated from community, that historical causality exerts its sway."[5] It is in the context of

----

[4]Ibid., p. 5.

[5]DM, in Coll., p. 255. Note the link between Hegelian-Marxist term 'alienation' and Lonergan's term 'bias' made by Lonergan in n. 10 to his lecture "Healing and Creating in History,' published in the same volume as TM, Bernard Lonergan: 3 Lectures, ed. and with introd. by R. Eric O'Connor (Montreal: Thomas More Institute, 1975) pp. 55-68: "I have written at great length on bias in Insight pp. 191-206; 218-242; 627-633; 688-693. In the Hegelian-Marxist tradition 'bias' is treated obliquely under the name of alienation." One could reverse Lonergan comment and say that the Hegelian-Marxist social analysis and ideology critique are treated obliquely by Lonergan under the name of 'bias'. Whatever is the case, the

Lonergan's argument as applied to his philosophy of history and culture that he elaborates the notion of the control of meaning. For besides the role of incarnate meaning informing the cultural infrastructure, there emerges reflection on meaning and value, and their subsequent controls, in the cultural superstructure [Figure 6]. In "Time and Meaning," Lonergan spells out the need for the analysis "of what precisely happens when a development occurs," and he affirms that it occurs "principally in the field of meaning."[6]

The changes in the field of meaning, however, are not the changes in meanings as concepts (which would in turn effect the shifts within a culture), but rather they are "changes in the meanings that are grasped and accepted."[7] In Lonergan's analysis of consciousness, the invariants of cultural change are the transcen-

---

section on bias in Insightt is of central importance, and, as Lonergan related to Robert Doran, S.J. in Pickering, Canada, in the last year of his life, it was composed prior to, and as a starting-point of, the rest of the book.

Fred Lawrence, in "Lonergan: a Tribute," Boston College Biweekly (Jan. 17. 1985), p. 8 writes the following interpretation of Lonergan's life-long work: "Today, especially in the light of both American Bishops' and the Lay Letters on the economy, the irony of a comment Lonergan made of his 130-paged manuscript [see reference in n. 82 infra] he laid aside in 1944 takes on a wistful note 'Now it is true that our culture cannot be accused of mistaken ideas on pure surplus income, as it has been defined in this essay. For on that precise topic, it has no ideas whatever.... Why does the proletariat today include almost everyone? Why is the control of industry in the hands of fewer and fewer? Radically, it is our own fault. We leave our affairs to others because we are too indolent and stupid to get to work and run them ourselves. The results are palpably ruinous. The system of free enterprise cannot survive if only a few practice free enterprise.'" See also nn. 36, 75, 80, 81, 85, 98, and 128 to this chapter infra.

[6]TM, p. 41.

[7]DM, in Coll., pp. 255-56.

CONSCIOUSNESS AS DIFFERENTIATED THROUGH CONTROLS OF MEANING AND VALUE

CONSCIOUSNESS/	SUBJECT/	CULTURAL STAGE
INFRASTRUCTURE/ Undifferentiated Consciousness:		
experience understanding judgement deliberation	spontaneous and mythic	incarnate and pre-systematic linguistic carriers of meaning; the basic opposition between the worlds of immediacy and those mediated and constituted by meaning in traditional culture, myth, magic, custom, common sense
SUPERSTRUCTURE/ Differentiated consciousness		
displacement to religious transcendence/religious subject		transcendental control of meaning--the basic opposition between the sacred and profane worlds
displacement to system/ theoretical subject		theoretical control of meaning--classicist culture; the basic opposition between the worlds of common sense and theory
displacement to interiority/ the rise of historical consciousness and critical subject		critical control of meaning--modernity and its basic opposition between the worlds of exteriority and interiority, and among the systematic horizon: scholarly, scientific, theological, and philosophic
displacement to method/ methodic subject		methodical control of meaning--post-modern functional differentiation and mediation of various discourses within an ongoing collaboration in the community of inquirers

Figure 6. Basic and reflexive mediation of cultural development

dental notions, and the variables are the categorial realizations, not vice versa.[8] The development of meaning in culture is immediate in historical consciousness, with its dynamism of conscious intentionality, and mediated in meaning and value controlling the common way of life.

It follows that the changes in the control of meaning that "mark off the great epochs in human history," are effected through differentiation of consciousness.[9] In another words, what Lonergan calls the "ongoing discovery of mind" in his Method In Theology, pertains to the culture's grasp and acceptance of the new criteria for the normative control of meaning and value-criteria that occurred in times when previously operative controls deteriorated or became ineffective. Lonergan speaks of three main stages of culture when these transpositions took place: the mythic and traditional cultures(s) exemplified by myth, magic, custom, and common-sense apprehension of the world; the classicist culture, controlled by systematic and theoretical exigencies of meaning; and the modern, with its shift to the critical exigence of interiority. Finally, the present crisis of culture calls for a new, methodical control of meaning.

I will discuss, first under B., traditional culture and its corresponding mythic consciousness; secondly, in section C., classicist culture with its theoretical control of meaning: (1) its underlying differentiation, and (2) displacement to system of mythic consciousness, (3) as it became operative in the Socratic maieutic and subsequent classicist notion of culture. Thirdly, in D., I will show the transposition and a crisis engendered by the cultural shift from classicism to modernity and its critical control of meaning. Fourthly, section E. will conclude and summarize the two converging, mediating and mediated, phases of methodological analysis, namely, historical operational development and the contemporary need for methodical control of meaning.

----

[8] MIT, pp. 11-12.

[9] Cf. DM, in Coll., p. 256.

B. Traditional Culture: Mythic Consciousness

On all cultural levels, the intersubjective, artistic, symbolic, and the pre-systematic linguistic, meanings are operative. These meanings mediate and constitute "the spontaneous substance of every culture."[10] They figure in the symbols of dreams, in art, and in the literature of primitive cultures. In low cultures, where consciousness remains undifferentiated through further operations, these meanings are yet unexamined by the therapist, literary analyst, or by the art critic. The elemental meanings and the ordinary languages, thus, pertain to their intersubjective basis in cultural infrastructure. Lonergan characterized the undifferentiated consciousness as "global":

> [It] is at once intellectual, moral and religious; it does not sort out different types of issues, specialize now in one type and later in another, seek the integration of separate, specialized developments.[11]

Undifferentiated consciousness does not discriminate between the procedures of common sense, and, hence, its explanatory power and its self-knowledge are rudimentary.[12] But even in this first stage of meaning, when consciousness is undifferentiated and operates in the realm of common sense, there are four cognitive, constitutive, effective, and communicative functions of meaning at work.[13] These functions are, however, not apprehended as separate. Lonergan gives an example of how insights into the intersubjective elemental meanings generate the names of plants and animals. These names can, then, be applied to clans and tribes in an analogical sense as some American sports teams take the names of Lions, Seals, or Bears.[14]

----

[10]GMC, in SC, p. 102.
[11]Cf. SC, p. 132.
[12]MIT, p. 84.
[13]Ibid., p. 89.
[14]Ibid.

Within the world of mythic consciousness, the cognitive and constitutive functions of meaning blend in myth. Myth narrates the world and the life-journey of the peoples as apprehended by the primitive culture. The efficient function of meaning intrudes into everyday practicality and results in magic. "Words bring about results not only by directing action but also by a power of their own which myth explains."[15]

Since mythic consciousness cannot distinguish the legitimate and illegitimate uses of the different functions of meaning, it apprehends and constructs the world symbolically.[16] Lonergan refers to Ernst Cassirer's Philosophy of Symbolic Forms,[17] when he describes the limitations imposed by the mythic consciousness: it cannot clearly separate representations and perceptions, wish and fulfillment, image, name and thing, dreaming and waking consciousness; and it is tolerant of contradictions. In another text, Lonergan describes Cassirer's example of the tribe that has never seen the villages of the tigers and the elephants, but it was convinced that such superior beings would have to live in very nice villages.[18]

Although the whole way of life in primitive cultures is surrounded and embedded in a symbolic, affect-laden world, narrated by myths and manipulated by magic, primitive people are intelligent and reasonable in their practical affairs. They grasp the vital, social, cultural, personal, and religious values in the symbolic, which they construct, narrate, and enact in their rituals. They communicate in story and dance about their fishing, hunting, sowing, reaping, being born, and dying. The earth is alive with generative power, but it also stands for the tomb; the sky opens the unbounded universe, but it also gives

---

[15]Ibid.

[16]Ibid., p. 306.

[17]Ernst Cassirer, The Philosophy Of Symbolic Forms, Vols. I-III (New Haven: Yale University Press, 1953, 1955, 1957); cf. MIT, p. 92.

[18]"An Interview with Bernard Lonergan, S.J.," in SC, pp. 225-26. [Hereafter abbreviated as IBL.]

rise to cosmological myths. Myths, sagas, legends, cosmogonies, and apocalypses express and effect the everyday practical tasks and focus the presence of mythic consciousness in the world about.

Common sense practicality develops beyond fruit-gathering, hunting, fishing, and gardening into

> large-scale agriculture with the social organization of the temple states and later of the empires of the ancient high civilizations in Egypt, Mesopotamia, Crete, the valleys of the Indus and the Hoan-ho, Mexico and Peru.[19]

The wealth and power of great ancient civilizations was substituted for the poverty of mythic consciousness; hence, that differentiation of common sense practicality still remained grounded upon the cosmological continuity between the order of society, the order of the universe, and that of the divine being.[20] Accordingly, ancient civilizations were able to utilize large populations and embark on

> great works of irrigation, vast structures of stone or brick, [build] armies and navies, complicated processes of bookkeeping, [develop] the beginnings of geometry, arithmetic, astronomy.[21]

As a style of practical intelligence, common sense is common to the human species, but in its content it

----

[19]MIT, p. 89; similar text as DM, in Coll., p. 257.

[20]MIT, p. 90; reference made by Lonergan to Eric Voegelin's Order And History, Vols. I-III (Louisiana State University Press, 1956), pp. 14 and 27 of Vol. I.

[21]Ibid., p. 89; cf. DM, in Coll., p. 257; on development of common sense practicality see Insight, pp. 207ff.

will be common to each village or regional culture, where "strangers appear strange...the more strangely they appear to speak and act."[22] Nevertheless, common sense, if left to its own expansion in practical affairs of divergent cultures, readily blends with common nonsense. Common sense practicality can become totalitarian in areas in which common sense does not have any competence. While both myth and magic are endowed with meaning and value, theirs is the meaning and value often gone astray:

> Just as the earth, left to itself, can put forth creapers and shrubs ... with such excessive abundance that there results an impenetrable jungle, so too the human mind, led by imagination and affect and uncontrolled by any reflexive technique, luxuriates in a world of myth with its glories to be achieved and its evils banished by the charms and magic.[23]

Indeed, mythic consciousness may differentiate and penetrate practical capabilities for the sake of severely restricting other possibilities of intelligent inquiry.[24] A note, then should be added on intention of truth in mythic consciousness.

For mythic consciousness, dreams are another way of attaining truth. Barden discovered that in one group of Australian aborigines dreams were not only well remembered, but that those with a high momentum of vivacity were "imbued by the waking subject with the intention of truth ...."[25] Something analogous pertains to intention of truth in myth. The dream reaches its aim in being dreamt; mythic intention of truth manifests itself in narrations or enactment of myths in a special context where the truth of the myths

----

[22]MIT, pp. 272.73.

[23]DM, in Coll., p. 258.

[24]Garrett Barden, in Language, Truth and Meaning, edited by Philip McShane (Notre Dame, Indiana: University of Notre Dame Press, 1972), p. 2.

[25]Ibid., p. 11.

is assumed.[26] As the dream overtakes the waking subject, so the affect-laden symbols in mythic subject overtake the imperatives of the intellect.[27] The real and true in mythic consciousness is mediated, constituted, effected, and communicated by the intense flow of affect, as these relate to symbols, objects, words, and rituals.[28] Barden points out the difficulty in <u>theoretic</u> grasp of mythic consciousness:

> Mythic consciousness is opaque to the mythic subject from which simple fact follows the notable conclusion that the theoretic grasp of a particular mythic consciousness, or of mythic consciousness in general, is not identical with that consciousness' grasp of itself.[29]

The subject <u>as</u> mythic does not know nor seek reflective criteria of truth and reality; for that question of truth and reality has not emerged as a possibility. Interestingly, besides talking about primitive cultures, Lonergan locates mythic consciousness in contemporary subjects and, in particular, in the philosopher and her apprehension of truth and reality. Mythic consciousness understands, but forgets, that experiencing, understanding, and judging have something to do with truth and reality. Mythic consciousness knows reality by touching, smelling, or by taking a good look. Its criteria of objectivity, if any, pertain to the 'already-out-there-now-real' or the 'already-in-here-now-real' of the infant's world of immediacy. The mythic subject assumes and takes for granted that the real and true are already grasped prior to any intelligent anticipation of the intelligible in questions; he thinks that reality, truth, objectivity and the good are reached by picture-thinking, that the now of the observer is the now of the observed.[30]

----

[26]Ibid.
[27]Ibid.
[28]Ibid.; cf. <u>Insight</u>, p. 538.
[29]Ibid.

M. Lamb comments on E. Neumann's Origins and History of Consciousness and compares the mythological origins of science in alchemy and magic, where mythic consciousness was projected into the physical universe, with the reversal in contemporary objectivism and scientism, where "the in-scape of mind is being treated according to the projected laws of the physical universe."[31] As Lonergan account of consciousness prescinds from any description by peering inwards, or by substituting a theory for one's experience, so also his 'deconstruction' of mythic consciousness and subsequent shifts to theoretical and to critical consciousness consist of heightening the mode of one's conscious operations. There is one's discovery marked by a "startling strangeness" yet to be made, namely:

> [T]hat there are two quite different realisms, that there is an incoherent realism, half animal and half human, that poses as a half-way house between materialism and idealism and, on the other hand, there is an intelligent and reasonable realism between which and materialism the half-way house is idealism.[32]

Lonergan's history of philosophy and his philosophy of history and culture, in Barden's words, offer "a dialectical movement of successive attempts to interrogate mythic consciousness," by breaking through

----

[30]IBL, in SC, pp. 218-19.

[31]Cf. E. Neumann, The origins And History of Consciousness, trans. by R. F. Hull (New York: Princeton University Press, 1970), pp. 210ff; cited in Lamb, History, Method, and Theology, p. 414.

[32]Insight, p. xviii. On the confusion between the criteria for a world of immediacy and the world mediated by meaning see Lonergan's DP, pp. 13-14: "Such inadvertence seems to be at the root of the confusion concerning objects and objectivity that has obtained in Western thought since Kant published his Critique of Pure Reason." Cf. also Coll., p. 208; and SC, pp. 77-78.

its limitations, or making that enclosure more secure.[33] In a similar manner, the individual subject, the philosopher, or the whole of cultural tradition are continually exposed to the exigencies of mythic controls of meaning and value and to the constraints of the mythic horizon.

Inversely, that is by 'deconstruction', breaking loose from myth and magic, in their ancient or contemporary ideological forms, is possible only through a thorough critique of the self and of cultural meanings in general. This critique, however, does not eliminate the symbolic, the artistic, and the mystical interplay of the signifiers with the signified in one's life; rather the critique empowers one's mediated return to immediacy or in Picasso's words, it endows one's ability to paint like a child with the controls of an adult.

To use another expression, Lonergan's methodological consideration of the operational development it unfolded throughout cultural history, and both his history of philosophy and philosophy of history, of science, and of culture, are carried in terms of 'decomposition', 'decentering', or 'deconstruction' of mythic subjectivity. Both Meno's questioning and Socrates' answers about the origin, the scope, and the goal of knowledge and moral life are principally about one's self-understanding. Lonergan does not exclude "the positive gains of behaviorism, Freudian psychoanalysis, or structuralist anthropology";[34] nevertheless, his interrogation and critique of the self are not merely a descent into the lowest structures that are expected to generate languages, myths, and discourses in general. Rather, his argument invites one's ongoing discovery of intelligence and of moral autonomy. It is in this sense that Lonergan's 'deconstruction' yields to upward development and not to complete banishment of the human subject.

----

[33] Garrett Barden, op. cit., p. 16.
[34] Lamb, op. cit., p. 16.

In the next section, I will begin with Socrates' interrogation of mythic consciousness and with the rise of the novel theoretical differentiation of consciousness.

C. Classicist Culture: Theoretical Control of Meaning

(1) The notion of differentiation of consciousness

As Piaget employed the notions of adaptation and of grouping of operations in order to distinguish the stages in the operational development of the child, so Lonergan broadened the notion of grouping of operations to account for the stages in cultural development.[35] First, the notion of grouping runs up against the limitations, for there emerge distinct horizons of mastered operations that do not group together. These "blocks" in grouping of operations give Lonergan the new terms of reference in his analysis of the development of meaning.[36]

----

[35]Mot, pp. 34-38.

[36]TM, p. 44. Compare different classifications of development: Piaget's, Lonergan's in Insight, ch. on Genetic Method, and the more concrete application of Piaget's research in Lonergan's study of development of meaning emerging explicitly in his work after 1959; cf. MoT, pp. 34-38.

There is a striking similarity between the classification of human development by Lonergan (appears between 1959-72) and by Jürgen Habermas (appears between 1976-81): both employ Piaget's developmental logic as the basis for the homology between ontogenesis and social evolution (On Lonergan's use of Piaget, see Chapter II of this study).

On Habermas' use of Piaget's developmental logic, see Anthony Giddens, "Jürgen Habermas," in The Return of Grand Theory in the Human Sciences edited by Quentin Skinner (Cambridge: Cambridge University Press, 1985), pp. 132-33; David Held, Introduction to Critical Theory: Horkheimer to Habermas (Berkeley: University of California Press, 1980), pp. 461-62 n. 89, 252, 267-295; Thomas McCarthy, The

Secondly, the limitations that arrest the operational development at a particular stage can be transcended only by a higher differentiation in the operator, which in human beings is affected through the _differentiation_ of the self-constitutive role of _consciousness_. The development from one stage of meaning to the next is promoted by the shift in the operational field, namely, through a novel control of meaning. By adverting to the significant transpositions in the control of meaning, it is possible to determine not only the meaning and value operative in different cultures, but also different worlds, the types of discourses that are available at a particular stage, the mode of learning, and within the stages of culture, also the progress, decline, and crisis of meaning.

Thirdly, Lonergan's classification of the stages of meaning according to common sense, theory, and interiority, though temporal, is not necessarily chronological; for there exists a possibility of a variety of differentiations of consciousness (and of their combinations) in higher cultures:

Large segments of population may

Critical Theory of Jürgen Habermas (Cambridge: the MIT Press, 1982), pp. 232-71; Jürgen Habermas, _The Theory of Communicative Action_ Vol. One _Reason and the Rationalization of Society_, transl. T. McCarthy (Boston: Beacon Press, 1984), pp. 3, 66-74, 194ff., 392, 416 n.43, 417, nn.44 and 49, and on moral development 254-62; Jürgen Habermas, _Communication and the evolution of Society_ (Boston: Beacon Press, 1979), pp. 69-177 ["Moral Development and Ego Identity," 69-94, "Historical Materialism and Development of Normative Structures," 95-125, "Towards a Reconstruction of Historical Materialism," 130-177, also McCarthy's Introduction, pp. xxi-xxiii], originally in J. Habermas, _Zur Rekonstruktion des Historischen Materialismus_ (Suhrkamp Verlag, 1976).

Consult nn. 5, 75, 80, 81, 85, 98, and 128 to this chapter.

> have undifferentiated consciousness though a culture is in the second or third stage, and many learned people may remain in the second stage when a culture has reached the third.[37]

Fourthly, the stages of meaning are employed as "ideal constructs,'" whereas the key to Lonergan's classification of mediation of meaning in culture is his notion of differentiated and undifferentiated consciousness--cultural superstructure built upon its cultural infrastructure.[38] So it is the differentiated consciousness, with its four (systematic, critical, transcendental, and methodical) _exigencies_ of meaning, that gives rise to different worlds or _realms_ of meaning. In other words, the significant relationship exists between the _mode_ of operations (exigencies) of meaning, that gives rise to different realms of meaning. In other words, the significant relationship exists between the _mode_ of operations (exigencies) and the _terms_ of meaning (realms), where the mode denotes the transposition of the prior stage into a higher type of operational development.

Fifthly, as the methodical analysis of human development in terms of the spontaneous subject and her operations runs into limitations or blocks in grouping of operations, so the _dynamism_, _structure_, and _specialization_ of consciousness provide us with _three fundamental oppositions_ that do not group together:[39]

> The dynamism of consciousness leads to a differentiation between operations that regard the _ultimate_, and on the other hand, _ordinary_ activity. The structure of consciousness leads to a distinction of the _inner_ and _outer_. A specialization of consciousness leads to a differentiation between the world of

----

[37]MIT, p. 85.

[38]Ibid.

[39]MoT, pp. 74-102; here Lonergan speaks of "three fundamental antitheses." Consult Figure 6 _supra_.

> common sense and the world of theory.... The fact that these basic fields of development cannot be grouped together to form a single homogeneous piece provides a basis for a logical division of development.... [Further] the logical division of fields provides a tool for distinguishing developments generally.... So the notion of mediation has a fundamental meaning insofar as any type of development opens the way to differentiating other worlds.[40]

Accordingly, the transcendental exigence of meaning differentiates consciousness into operations regarding the worlds of the profane and of the sacred; the systematic exigence divides conscious operations into the worlds of theory and common sense; and the critical exigence effects the transitions between the worlds of exteriority and interiority (cf. Fig. 6).

Finally, Lonergan's notion of the methodical exigence of meaning arises when one is able to operate on the operations themselves. Method, in Lonergan's sense, is the final liberation of the initial theorem of mediation. For the methodically self-appropriated subject will be able to mediate among the systematic, critical, and transcendental exigencies of meaning and the complex variations of differentiated and undifferentiated consciousness. Nevertheless, the methodical exigence will not replace the special methods in each department of theory, nor the variety of the common ways of living. Rather, it will be able to mediate not only the historical proliferation of the myriads of common sense worlds, or of the theoretical contexts of meaning, but also the operations mastered by the natural and human sciences, scholarship, history, philosophy, and theology. Lonergan's methodological analysis, then, divides into its mediating phase, that considers the past, and a mediated phase, that opens up to the future.[41] [Figure 7.]

----

[40]Ibid., pp. 100-106 (italics mine).

The methodical exigence pays attention to both phases by "showing how they can possess a dynamic interdependence and unity."[42] Thus, method, in mediating the differentiation and specialization of historical consciousness, is able to draw functional distinctions and divisions among the horizons and fields of mastered operations and, consequently, "to curb one-sided totalitarian ambitions" of either the common sense or of the different functional specialties.[43]

MEDIATION	EXIGENCIES OF MEANING	FUNDAMENTAL OPPOSITIONS
[Past] Mediating Phase	transcendental systematic critical	[Worlds of] profane/ sacred common sense/ theory exteriority/interiority
[Future] Mediated Phase	methodical	common sense--theory--interiority--transcendence--natural and human sciences, history, scholarship, philosophy, theology, etc.

Figure 7. Mediating and mediated phases of method

(2) Displacement to system

In "Dimensions of Meaning" Lonergan recalls Karl Jaspers' Origin and Goal of History:

> According to Jaspers, there is an axis on which the whole of human history turns; that axis lies between the years 800 and 200 B.C.; during that period in Greece, in Israel, in Persia, in India, in

----

[41]MIT, p. 144.
[42]Ibid., p. 145.
[43]Ibid., p. 137.

> China, man became of age; he set aside the dreams and fancies of childhood, he began to face the world as perhaps it is.[44]

When the first differentiation of consciousness occurs, one learns to talk; when the ordinary and literary languages develop, one is able to portray "men in all their complexity."[45] It is this second development that effects the emergence of logos from mythos:

> So it is that in Western culture, for the past twenty-four centuries, the movement associated with the name of Socrates and the achievement of fourth-century Athens have been regarded as a high point, as a line of cleavage, as the breaking through of a radically new era in the history of man.[46]

The Socratic maieutic, the art of definition, emerged at a time when people (in ancient Greece) became discontented with the common sense and mythic controls of meaning handed down through generations in everyday culture. Socrates engaged Athenians in an experiment which had to do with their apprehension of meaning. His enterprise was, however, prepared by preceding Homeric reflections on knowledge, by Xenophanes' critique of the anthropomorphic representations of the gods, by Heraclitean insistence on a logos within all things, and by Parmenides' and Zeno's arguments against the senses.[47]

Socrates challenged not only the myths and accepted customs of Athenian society, but also the eloquence and scepticism of the Sophists. He demanded

----

[44]DM in Coll., p. 258; cf. Insight, pp. 575-76.

[45]PGT, p. 4; on early development of language see pp. 2-4, and MIT, pp. 86-88; on language development in biblical and theological contexts see MIT, pp. 305-308.

[46]DM, in Coll., p. 258; cf. Insight, pp. 575-76.

[47]PGT, pp. 2-3; MIT, pp. 90-92.

universal definitions of virtues and wanted to _know_ what knowledge _is_. He knew what the universal definition consisted of, but was unable to find the answers to his quest. While common sense does not acknowledge the importance of verbal, notional, and real distinctions, Socrates was not able to draw them.[48]

These distinctions may stand either for mere _names_, or for the _meanings_ of words, or for the _realities_ meant. But these realities are not known merely by the senses, but also by understanding and judgement. Thus it is in judgement that the intelligible _spheres of being_ are distinguished. Now Socrates' effort to safeguard meaning and value resulted in differentiation of the spontaneous, everyday level, and the secondary, reflexive level of meaning.[49] Although the Athenians knew well the difference between courage, justice, and injustice, self-control, knowledge, and ignorance, neither they nor Socrates himself were able to produce the definitions sought. The Delphic Oracle about Socrates was at the same time true and ironical: "[H]e was the wisest because he at least knew that he did not know."[50]

Despite the irony of the Socratic ignorance, the very question what am I doing when I know? was made possible with Socrates' shift to the _intellectual pattern of experience_. For it is in this pattern that one's intellectual wonder and, consequently, one's desire to know promote the emergence of the _systematic exigence of meaning_.

Plato, "at a certain stage" in his thought supposed that there are two really distinct worlds of transcendent Forms and of mutable appearances.[51] Aristotle, on the other hand, settled for two approaches to one world. So there is the latter's theory about what is prior in itself but posterior to us and, everyday knowledge, what is prior for us and posterior in itself.[52]

----

[48]MIT, p. 93.
[49]DM, in _Coll_., p. 256.
[50]Ibid., p. 257.
[51]MIT, p. 95.

CONSCIOUSNESS AS DIFFERENTIATED THROUGH CONTROLS OF MEANING AND VALUE

Aristotle was able to define virtue and vice in his Nichomachean Ethics, because "he moved beyond the ordinary language of common sense and the refinements brought to it by literary development into systematic thinking.'[53] He was able to distinguish the primitive and the derived terms, and their relations, list the meanings of words and group them according to different categories and, thus, develop a logical system.

The context of the Aristotelian system was grounded on a metaphysics. His two approaches to the one world are, however, not the same as a distinction between common sense and theory; rather, they are the difference between necessity and contingence.[54] Accordingly, Aristotle's metaphysics provided the basic terms for the natural sciences, for the account of the soul, for his notion of object, and it grounded his analysis of motion and rest. Necessity was a key notion to his conception of science as found in Posterior Analytics. Science for Aristotle was true, certain knowledge of causal necessity; it was based on a deduction from the first, that is, self-evident and necessary principles. The normative in the Aristotelian system was the universal and abstract: knowledge of things in their essences and properties as determined through the formal, material, efficient, and final causes.

Thus, Greek discovery of the systematic control of meaning was stabilized in the Aristotelian corpus which (1) provided a logic of terms, relations, and inferences; (2) was grounded on a metaphysics with its account of the things best known in themselves; (3) defined science as based on logical and metaphysical normativity of the first principles; and (4) elaborated psychology with a metaphysical account of the soul and of human nature.

The difference between reality as known by common sense and by theory is not that common sense is

----

[52]Ibid.
[53]PGT, p. 4 (italics mine).
[54]MIT, p. 95.

concrete and theory is abstract. Rather, "there is a difference in the end, the object, the language, and the structure of consciousness of the two."[55] Common sense is concerned with practicality, with things as they are related to us; it uses ordinary language, and its intellectual operations are just part of the whole structure of consciousness. On the other hand, the theoretical subject is dominated by the intellectual desire to know; theory considers things as they are related to one another, and it says in technical language what otherwise would require many pages in the ordinary or literary languages. While one can proceed from things as related to us to things as related to one another, and vice versa, the two are opposite; and only the theoretical subject initially can make that distinction. Aristotle was able to do what Socrates began in search for universal definitions, because the classical _Organon_ provided a new systematic structure, which was lacking before common sense.

(3) The classicist notion of culture

The systematic control of meaning, which originated in Greece, resulted not only in a theoretical apprehension of the universe, in a systematic way of learning, in development of technical vocabulary, and in the rise of the philosophic community. It also led to the development of classical (or classicist) culture. Classical culture designed its own "canons of art, its literary forms, its rules of correct speech, its norms of interpretation, its way of thought, its manner of philosophy ... its concept of law, its moral standards, it methods of education...." [56]

Classicist cultural superstructure arose as a response to the need for effective control of meaning--the _ethos_ informing the common way of life. The rise of the theoretical differentiation of consciousness, thus, led to a collective thematization of culture in various academic disciplines. For undifferentiated consciousness, an academic development is not only considered irrelevant, but it is wholly impossible. On the other hand, for differentiated consciousness, the

----

[55]MoT, p. 87.
[56]DM, in _Coll_., pp. 258-9.

reflection on, and the subsequent control of meaning are a matter of survival:

> It follows more or less inevitably that the further any movement spreads and the longer it lasts, the more it is forced to reflect on its own proper meaning, to distinguish itself from other meanings, to guard itself against aberration.[57]

As Lonergan stresses in one of his lectures, "the community has to come to a point when it wants to understand itself and has to understand itself to go on. . . ."[58] It is at this cross-section of wanting and needing to understand, i.e., within the intellectual pattern of experience, that "there emerges that shift towards system, which was named by Georg Simmel, die Wendung zur Idee."[59]

Lonergan remarks that neither Aristotle nor Aquinas provided their systematic works with necessary first principles: "They were content to do what they could."[60] Later Scholasticism, however, developed the initial logical context of operations on propositions to "a fully metaphysical context' of verbal, notional, and real distinctions, where the real distinction applied both to an ordinary case, or, analogically, to the divine mystery.[61] That fully self-conscious Scholasticism was influenced by developed common sense, by religion, arts, and literary styles, but also "by the slight dose of systematic meaning found in Greek councils."[62]

----

[57]MIT, p. 139.

[58]The quote is from the recordings of Lonergan's DMT cited by Dennis Daly Klein in "Dimensions of Culture in the Thought of Bernard Lonergan" (unpublished Ph.D. dissertation, Department of Philosophy, Boston College, April 1975), p. 193.

[59]MIT, p. 139.

[60]PGT, p. 6.

[61]MIT, p. 308.

[62]Ibid., p. 309.

In contrast to Aristotle and Aquinas, in fourteenth and fifteenth century Scholasticism, their rigorous concern with necessary truth, with what God could do absolutely, or may be expected to do without falling into a contradiction, brought about scepticism, verbalism, and later decadence.[63] The verbalism of the later scholastic theories led to a proliferation of extrinsicist conceptualism marked by extreme logicality, a historical immobilism, and abstract universalism of the normative controls of meaning. Klein, in his doctoral dissertation, notes that this development parallels on the higher level of intelligence the "proclivity of mythical consciousness...."[64] Accordingly, what Lonergan says about mythic consciousness is applicable to the human intellect when uncontrolled by a meaningful reflexive control of meaning.[65]

As various mythic cultures were succeeded in the West by a single classicist culture which lasted from the fifth century B.C. and "breathed life and form" into the civilizations of Greece and Rome, Middle Age, and Renaissance Europe, so this culture gradually collapsed, was virtually destroyed during the French revolution and today, "nearly everywhere, it is dead and almost forgotten."[66] The classicist, normative view of its own cultural hegemony and superiority over the barbarians was handed down to posterity in liberal arts education, in its cultural tastes, in skills, ideals and virtues, in immortal classics of literature, in art, and in its perennial philosophy. "Classicist education was a matter of models to be imitated, of ideal characters to be emulated, of eternal verities and universally valid laws."[67] The classical ideal of a civilized, cultured human person was not a specialist, but "a universal man," the *uomo universale*.

----

[63]Ibid., p. 311; PGT, p. 6.
[64]Klein, *op. cit.*., p. 345; on conceptualism in Scotus, see Lonergan's VWIA, n. 122, pp. 25-6; also his *Sub*., in SC; on change of concepts see *Insight*, pp. 736-39; and MIT, pp. 302; 325.
[65]Cf. DM, in *Coll*., p. 258.
[66]Ibid., p. 259.
[67]MIT, p. 301.

Lonergan recollects about his own education in Montreal, in 1918. He went to a boarding school, organized on a Jesuit Renaissance model with some few modifications: "So that I can speak of classical culture as something I was brought up in and gradually learned to move out."[68]

There existed one culture, "culture with a capital C; a normative notion of culture."[69] The cognitive, constitutive, effective, and communicative functions of meaning were all controlled and occurred <u>within</u> the same, one classical self-understanding. Accordingly, the classicist is no pluralist.[70] The classicist mind-set considers the circumstances as being nearly accidental to the immutable root of the classicist normativity. What is said of the specific natures of things applies as well to human nature: It remains the same whether one is asleep or awake, moron or intelligent, child or adult. The classicist culture had a blind spot towards the concrete, the empirical, the historical, and the pluralist. Thus, "neither classicist culture nor Aristotelian thought inculcated the principle that unified world-views are subject to notable changes."[71]

In the next section, I will address the shift from

----

[68]Cf. SC, pp. 209-10.

[69]Ibid.

[70]MIT, p. 310.

[71]Ibid., p. 315. Cf. Bernard Lonergan, "(Towards) A Definition Of Education," unpublished draft (Regis College, Lonergan Centre: Toronto, Feb.9, 1949); by courtesy of Fr. F. Crowe, S.J. [Hereafter abbreviated as TDE.] In this draft, there is a cryptic note that testifies to Lonergan's <u>early</u> interest in the transposition of culture: "Dialectical Artefact: <u>a</u>' make a machine, build a house, result fixed settled. Civilization is something in perpetual movement. <u>b</u>' Nature of movement. What is wrong with classicism: there exists a beautiful ideal valid for all places and times. Magnificent classicism; France of grand siècle: tried to freeze things and ended in French Revolution; big thaw ... practical." [TDE, P. 2.]

the classicist to modern culture.

D. The Transposition of Classicism and a Crisis of Modernity: Critical Control of Meaning

To begin, I quote again from Lonergan's experience as a teacher:

> I taught theology for twenty-five years under impossible conditions. It was that the whole setup of the school was predicated upon things that were fine in the sixteenth century, but you could not use modern scholarship properly the way things are lined up.[72]

Therein lie, then, Lonergan's key experiences of the classicist control of meaning, its decline and breakdown, and of the subsequent crisis of culture. To name just a few: 1918 in boarding school, in Montreal, and his later teaching in Regency in 1930-31;[73] the "entry of science" into Lonergan's long search while working on Insight (1926-53);[74] reading of Piaget's experimental analysis of child development (1959); his study of the German historical school (after 1963); and the problematic of meaning and value in his preliminary lectures for his Method in Theology (1962-72).[75]

----

[72]PGT, p. 15; reference is apparently to Lonergan's teaching at the Gregorian University in Rome.

[73]CAM, p. 9.

[74]Ibid., pp. 42-43.

[75]On development of Lonergan's notion of culture, see SC, pp. 209-10; on Piaget, see pp. 211, 222; on classical treatises, see p. 211; on Insight and its purpose see p. 213; on meaning and value see pp. 220-21; on shift in Lonergan's thought, see the introduction by Ryan and Tyrrell. Note: in light of the text supra in n. 73 to this ch., it seems that the difference between the early and the late Lonergan is not that radical, but rather that his preoccupation with cultural transpositions exemplifies continuous deepening of his early insights and interests in culture and economics.

CONSCIOUSNESS AS DIFFERENTIATED THROUGH CONTROLS OF MEANING AND VALUE

Lonergan's entry into the dilemmas of modernity, its classical roots, the causes of its emergence, and its post-modern bewilderment had principally one ulterior purpose that "regards neither primitives nor Greeks but ourselves."[76]

Lonergan clarifies his reasons for referring to Karl Jaspers' view of history by pointing out that there emerged a new axial period in modern culture, i.e., a shift in culture's own self-understanding. The problem of contemporary culture can be illustrated by an image of a slum: There are multiple and complex horizons that emerged within modernity, but there is not yet mature and novel self-understanding. "The slum is an accumulation of unsolved problems. Slums are slums not because of locality but because of people who dwell in them."[77] One can think of the slum as a negation of regional culture,[78] when it exemplifies the failure of our industrial society. But the slum is not a result of merely social or vital factors. Rather, the problem of the slum lies in "the breakdown of human dignity, human cohesion and human standards....[It} is a consequence of the attempt in recent centuries to remake man."[79]

The breakdown of culture is the outcome primarily of the eclipse of the prior control of meaning. To-day's crisis, in Lonergan's analysis, is not princi-

---

Critique of economic theory and praxis is an underlying current of Lonergan's work in the areas of philosophy (Insight) and theology (MIT). On the Hegelian-Marxist immanent critique of alienation, see n. 5 supra and nn. 80 and 81 infra; consult also nn. 36, 85, 98, and 128 to this chapter.

[76]DM, in Coll., p. 258.

[77]TDE, p. 5.

[78]PE, p. 241; the term "regional culture" is taken by Lonergan from Christopher Dawson who was one of the earliest influences of on Lonergan's analysis of culture; cf. CAM, pp. 9ff.

[79]Ibid. The phrase, "attempts to remake man," cited supra perhaps refers to Lonergan's statement that contributions of philosophy have not done little to make our lives unlivable during the past 200 years.

pally social, vital, or even a religious one--it is a crisis in the mediation of meaning in culture. Thus, both Lonergan's economic manuscript, Essay in Circulation Analysis,[80] and his historical study of meaning in terms of the operational development are closely linked. Although I must prescind from attempting to compare Marx's and Lonergan's social analysis, i.e., interrelationships between the basis and superstructure in Marx, or infra- and superstructure in Lonergan, it is worth noting the two points concerning Marx found in Lonergan's 1949 draft about "the basic factor in dialectic of civilization: (1) Marx: spent life mainly in the British museum.... (2) Marxist: wrong because ideas and will produce the situations."[81]

What Lonergan seems to credit Marx with (while still using faculty psychology which he later abandons) is his effort to understand; Lonergan, however, rejects the contention that it is the social that determines the emergence of the cultural, that the meaning of the social is incarnate in the cultural infrastructure, or that it is the historical that eclipses the subject. Rather, it is the cultural superstructure arising upon its elemental meanings in the cultural infrastructure, Lonergan holds, which effects the changes within

---

[80]Bernard Lonergan, Essay in Circulation Analysis(Boston: Boston College, 1944, 1978, 1980, 1982), unpublished MS and a supplement to lectures on economics held by Lonergan in the last years of his teaching career. On the link among macroeconomics, the dialectic of history, and theology see p. 2 of this MS. [Hereafter abbreviated as ECA.]

[81]TDE, p. 4 art. d' and b'; here Lonergan refers to A.N. Whitehead with respect to the latter's treatment of the influence of medieval universities on the modern world in his Science And The Modern World. On Marx see Insight, pp. 217, 227, 233, 235, 238, 241, 374, and 742; also consult nn. 5, 36, 75, 80, 85, 98, and 128 to this chapter. Compare Lonergan's transposition of the orthodox Marxist themes of the base-superstructure and of alienation-emancipation and J. Habermas' critical transposition of those themes in hisReconstruction of Historical Materialism; consult n. 36 to this chapter and figures 6 and 7.

cultures. In the concluding paragraph of "Dimensions of Meaning," Lonergan accounts for the contemporary appearance of "a solid right" and "a scattered left." They both appear within the context of the cultural breakdown of classicism, and they both "run counter to classical expectations." The former "is determined to live in a world that no longer exists"; the latter is "captivated by now this, now that new possibility."[82]

The extremes of right and left are perhaps what Lonergan refers to when he speaks of the contemporary revival of mythical consciousness in one type of myth and magic in "up-to-date myth of ideology and the hypnotic, highly effective magic of thought control."[83] What will count, then, is one's self-appropriation of his/her operational development:

> Rational self-consciousness is a peak above the clouds. Intelligent and reasonable, responsible and free, scientific and metaphysical, it stands above romantic spontaneity and the psychological depths, historical determinism and social engineering, the disconcerted existential subject and the undeciphered symbols of the artist and the modernist.[84]

Again, what will count is a collaborative effort to understand:

> [A] perhaps not numerous center, big enough to be at home in both the old and the new; painstaking enough to work out one by one the transitions to be made, strong enough to refuse half-measures and insist on complete solutions even though it has to wait.[85]

----

[82]DM, in Coll., pp. 266-67.
[83]Ibid., p. 259.
[84]OPI, p. 3.
[85]DM, in Coll., p. 267.

There are five transpositions from classicist to contemporary culture suggested by Lonergan:

> [F]rom logic to method; from science as conceived in the Posterior Analytics to science as it is conceived today; from the metaphysics of the soul to the self-appropriation of the subject; from an apprehension of man in terms of human nature to an apprehension of man through human history; and from first principles to transcendental method.[86]

While Lonergan suggests the transpositions, he also rejects the "half-measure' that have appeared concomitantly with the rise of modernity. Besides his lifelong concern with economics and alternative social analysis (which stand at the beginning and the close of his career), there are three topics related to mediation of meaning in culture that entered into Lonergan's work, namely the death of God, the death of the subject, and an end of history. He partially affirms a possibility of all three themes insofar as one remains with merely the negative insight ('deconstruction') that a metaphysics of the soul apprehended in terms of the ahistorical, simply given, or immediately present human nature, and the first principles of the classicist deductivist system, broke down, and with them also vanished the classicist normativity as a meaningful control of meaning:

----

[86]Bernard Lonergan, "The Future of Thomism," in SC, p. 50. [Hereafter abbreviated as FT.]

(The requirement for a "not numerous center" and "complete solutions" in the above transpositions is perhaps comparable to the effort of Critical Theory: it avoids the oversights of vulgar Marxism or naive Leftist activism--the ones critiqued by Lonergan--and the oversights of the post-Modern dissolution of human autonomy and history and the general bias towards the status quo of consumer capitalism or of scholastic, i.e. uncritical, Thomism). Consult nn. 5, 36, 75, 80, 81, 98, and 128 to this chapter.

CONSCIOUSNESS AS DIFFERENTIATED THROUGH CONTROLS OF MEANING AND VALUE

> Just what is man? Answers ... have been worked out by theologians and scientists, by politicians and sociologists, by biologists and psychologists, by ethnologists and economists. But not only do the many answers not agree, not only is there lacking some generally acceptable principle that would select one and reject the others, but even within the specialized fields there seems to be no method that can confront basic issues without succumbing to individual temperament and personal evaluations.[87]

Lonergan's argument, then, does not prove that in the subject as subject we shall find "the evidence, norms, invariants, principles for a critique of horizons"; but it proves that unless we can find them there, we shall not find them at all.[88]

As "the Greek miracle" of displacement to theory "had its price" in a "second withdrawal from the world of immediacy" of mythic consciousness[89] establishing the opposition between common sense and theory, so the modern miracle of the new empirical science, modern languages, nation states, and the immense proliferation of theories with their specializations, must have its price in the third withdrawal from immediacy. It is in this <u>third withdrawal from a world of mythic consciousness</u>, that rational, responsible, and historical self-consciousness mediates common sense and theory by interiority.

Now the "first price" paid is illustrated by the opposition between common sense and theory. Let us take Lonergan's own example and talk about the giraffe.[90] The father and the son go to the zoo, and

----

[87]OPI, p. 5.

[88]NE, p. 28.

[89]Bernard Lonergan, "The Dehellenization Of Dogma," in SC, p. 20 [Hereafter abbreviated as DOD.]

both take a look at the giraffe. They both see the motley neck, the head, the trunk, the tail, the legs, and the color of the skin and affirm it to be a giraffe. "A biologist looks at the same animal; he thinks of it as a unity of systems ... a locomotive ... a digestive ... a vascular ... a nervous system...."[91] What is a giraffe? "A unity of systems that regard immediately organs: but mediately cells, chemical and subatomic processes, etc."[92] The biologist's giraffe is the unity-identity-whole, not as related to us, but as many interrelations that cannot be imagined.

The price paid is that the two worlds do not integrate, and so there is a time for theorizing and a time for small talk. These two different languages, two types of subjects, two communities of everyday and of theoretical discourses. There may arise suspicions of the theorists against the criteria of the common sense person, and of the ordinary person against the uselessness of the theorist. Another of Lonergan's favorite examples is Eddington's two tables. The one is brown, smooth, solid, with four legs, and hard to push. The other is a complex of unimaginable electrons and wavicles, mostly an empty space.[93] The two are opposite, they do not form a group. One can be a scientist during the day and a parent when at home. Moreover, this opposition can be illustrated in the Kantian contrast between the phenomenal and the noumenal worlds, Aquinas's "hymns and his systematic theology," and "Galileo's secondary and primary qualities."[94] Briefly, a dynamic cognitive structure in spontaneous or theoretical apprehension of the world is analogous to "two different kinds of clock," two different types of whole exemplified as mediation of knowing with other patterns of experience and mediation by a pure desire to know of the intellectual pattern of experience.[95]

90TM, p. 44; cf. CRIS, pp. 36-7.
91Ibid.
92Ibid., p. 45.
93UB, pp. 10, 77; cf. MIT, pp. 84, 258, 274; also CRIS, pp. 36-7.
94MIT, p. 258.
95CRIS, pp. 35-7.

CONSCIOUSNESS AS DIFFERENTIATED THROUGH CONTROLS OF MEANING AND VALUE

There is a second price to be paid when philosophy has to "migrate from the world of theory" and find a new basis. For, as science develops, it gives up most of the claims to necessity, certainty, causality, and truth expected in the Aristotelian ideal of science. Modern science is probable, is hypothetical, and relies on verification of possibilities, i.e., not of what always must be so, but what in fact is. It attends to data rather than to things, to correlations rather than to causes.

On the other hand, the success of modern science "lends color to *totalitarian ambitions*, and science conceives its goal as the full explanation of all phenomena."[96] The second price paid is, then, the dilemma between *relativism* and *totalitarianism* of horizons. Within this dilemma, there arise questions about the meaning of truth, about relations of common sense to theory, and vice versa, about methods in human sciences, about historicity of theories and of their criteria of objectivity. It is at this cross-section in cultural development that the desire and need for self-understanding calls for the transposition to the third stage of meaning, i.e., the *critical subject* within the world of interiority represents a distinct stage in the development of meaning. "But while the transition from common sense to theory introduces us to entities that we do not directly experience, the transition from common sense and theory to interiority promotes us from *consciousness of self* to *knowledge of self*."[97]

No amount of theory, common sense talk, or of introspection can promote one to self-appropriation of one's conscious operational development. The critical exigence of meaning does not group with the operations performed in the world of immediacy, with those in the world mediated and constituted by the basic carriers of meaning, or with those mastered by the theorist. For interiority is a world of its own: it regards not the data of sense but of consciousness.

----

[96]MIT, p. 259 (italics mine).
[97]Ibid.

MEDIATION OF DECONSTRUCTION

My thesis is that Lonergan, in going beyond mere logical coherence of systematic meaning, engenders a project of 'deconstruction', but in quite another sense his argument, unlike Derrida's attack on logic and its logocentric metaphysics of presence, _is a genuine and legitimate ad hominem from human operational development_.[98] Lonergan's argument is precisely _ad hominem_ in the sense in which a logician might find it to be fallacious, minus the logician's own disingenuousness, which is subject to 'deconstruction', sublation, and mediation by critical interiority.

Lonergan's argument does not rest on deductive proofs, because the proofs pertain to theoretical systems, which themselves remain unproved. To illustrate the limitations of the ongoing theoretical contexts, one must consider the collapse of determinism

----

[98]In my treatment of the _argumentum ad hominem_ in relation to Lonergan's methodology I am drawing upon Mark Morelli's contribution to the 1984 Boston College "Lonergan Workshop," in his paper "Reversing the Counter-Position: _The Argumentum Ad Hominem_ in Philosophic Dialogue." The paper is published in _Lonergan Workshop_, edited by Fred Lawrence, Vol. 6 (Atlanta, GA: Scholars Press, 1986), pp. 195-230.

An interesting parallel of Lonergan's _ad hominem_ exists with Karl Marx's "Towards a Critique of Hegel's _Philosophy of Right_: Introduction" in David McLellan, ed., _Karl Marx: Selected Writings_ (Oxford: Oxford University Press, 1977), p. 69: "The weapon of criticism cannot ... supplant the criticism of weapons; material force must be overthrown by material force. But theory, too, will become material force as soon as it seizes the masses. _Theory is capable of seizing the masses as soon as its proofs are ad hominem and its proofs are ad hominem as soon as it is radical. To be radical is to grasp the matter by the root. But for man the root is man himself."_ (Italics mine.) It is in this sense that in the Preface I call Lonergan's argument _radical_ rather than the _tamed_ one; the "radical Lonergan" grasps the matter by the root, i.e., through human operational development towards authentic freedom. Consult nn. 5, 36, 75, 80, 81, 85, and 128 to this chap.

in 19th century physics and economics, the discovery of non-Euclidean geometry, of Quantum mechanics, Keynesian economics, and of Gödel's limitations of any deductivist system:

> [I]f one accepts the theorem propounded by Kurt Gödel, one will conclude with him that realizations of the deductivist ideal are either trivial or incomplete or incoherent.... In brief, like the mortician, the logician achieves a steady state only temporarily. The mortician prevents not the ultimate but only the immediate decomposition of the corpse. In similar fashion the logician brings about, not the clarity, the coherence and the rigor that will last forever, but only the clarity, the coherence and the rigor that will bring to light the inadequacy of current views and thereby give rise to the discovery of a more adequate position.[99]

The corpse, which Lonergan emphatically links with the illusion of logical techniques (embalmments denying an imminent death), is the logical discourse, itself subject to 'deconstruction', and not the logician as operating human subject.

Lonergan proposes a third context for a systematic rational discourse based neither on a metaphysics nor on an empirical science, but grounded in basic, recurrent operations and relations of conscious intentionality, and in derived terms and relations that are exhibited in the operations of mythic consciousness, in common sense, in mathematics, in natural and human sciences, in the operations of psychoanalysis and those of their patients, in the operations of scholars, historians, philosophers, theologians, structuralists, and the tenets of deconstruction.[100] His argument for

----

[99]On Gödel's theorem see PGT, p. 6 (italics mine).

this third context of rational discourse is a genuine ad hominem: it does not appeal to illegitimate reasons irrelevant to the argument, but, on the contrary, it affirms that genuine objectivity is the fruit of authentic subjectivity. As Derrida may not be an author of his deconstruction (though he might be a victim of his own project), similarly, there is no such thing as a Lonerganian argument.[101] Lonergan's argument is at best an invitation to the hypothetical interlocutor to discover himself as consciously, intelligently, reasonably, and responsibly operating. It is only in this sense of one's self-discovery that the argumentum ad hominem can be freed from the logician's charge of irrelevance and illegitimacy. Thus the stone rejected has become the cornerstone.

But the argumentum ad hominem as a philosophical methodology can be rejected, even if genuine, on an a priori ground as being irrelevant "from idealist tendencies no less than from linguistic analysis."[102] There exists, then, the possibility of death of the subject. The human subject can be decomposed like the reality in Picasso's "Les Demoiselles d'Avignon," it can be remade as in Rodin's "Thinker," or in Le Corbusier's architecture for the modern age.[103] The subject can be redefined through the "extrascientific opinions of scientists," or by the "philosophic assumptions of historians."[104]

Lonergan's argument concerns the meaning and value of living and operating. His is a question about the relevance of life within the post-modern breakdown of the cultural superstructure. For, meaning and value can be opposed by their negation, by nihilism.[105] The

----

[100]Ibid., pp. 6-8.

[101]IBL, in SC, p. 213.

[102]MIT, p. 262.

[103]Cf. Pablo Picasso, "Les Demoiselles d'Avignon" (New York: The Museum of Modern Art, 1907). This painting marks Picasso's transition to cubism. On Le Corbusier, see Christian Norberg-Schulz, Genius Loci: Towards a Phenomenology of Architecture (New York: Rizzoli International Publications, 1079), pp. 191ff.

[104]Cf. MIT, p. 318.

[105]Cf. TM, p. 39.

'archeology' and 'genealogy' of human subjectivity, after displacement and decentering of all layers within human consciousness and subconsciousness, might declare that not only God but also the subject and human history are dead. The truth, then, that portrays men and women as they are rejects as meaningless the human claim for the primacy of intelligence and the ongoing discovery of one's own historical self-mediation. Lonergan's argument, however, does not go against the logical incoherence of the hypothetical nihilist; for the latter still could feel justified in eclipsing both the primacy of intelligence and of historical continuity of the subject. Rather, the argument rests on the incoherence _of_ the operations _with_ the reports on the human condition and its history.

To illustrate Lonergan's account of historical consciousness in contrast to the positions he would find incoherent on the basis of _operational performance_, let me briefly quote from Michel Foucault's post-structuralist interpretative essay on Nietzsche's conception of genealogy in relation to history. In _Language, Counter-Memory, Practice_, Foucault brings up three counterpoints to the notion of historical consciousness: the first is parodic, farcial, directed against reality and the theme of history as reminiscence or recognition; the second is dissociative, directed against identity, continuity or representative of a tradition; the third is sacrificial, directed against truth and history as knowledge.[106] The purpose of history, as guided by genealogy in the Nietzschean sense, is "not to discover the roots of our identity but to commit itself to its dissipation."[107] Against "antiquarian history," genealogy as counter-memory reveals the _heterogeneity of systems_, which

> masked by the self, inhibit the formation of any form of identity.... [History] is no longer a

----

[106]Michel Foucault, _Language, Counter-Memory, Practice_, selected essays and interviews, trans. by Donald F. Bouchard and Sherry Simon (Ithaca, New York: Cornell University Press, 1977), pp. 160-64.

[107]Ibid., p. 162.

> question of judging the past in the name of a truth that only we can possess in the present; but risking the destruction of the subject who seeks knowledge in the endless deployment of the will to knowledge.[108]

Lonergan might agree on many of the above points that bring forth the tragedy of human beings as they are, or the tragedy of culture that has lost or completely negated meaning. But he would contend that insisting on those points as normative manifests, besides the displacement of the mythic, theoretical, and critical subject, implicit interrogation of consciousness for the sake of securing meaning and, thus, denies the very thing it wants to expose. For Foucault appeals to experience, his understanding of that experience, judgement of his understanding, deliberation upon the meaning and value of the conclusions drawn, and communication of his findings to a broad human intersubjective community. There is, then, operative a rift between an implicit definition of Foucault's performance and his explicit thematization of the problematic of meaning, value, and their reflexive controls.

While post-modern language finds its home in the absurd, senseless, or heterogeneous, Lonergan enters these very themes with his invitation to the dialectical reversal of what he calls basic counter-positions on truth, reality, objectivity, and the good, as these were defined in Chapter I *supra*. The reversal of basic counter-positions highlights the rift between the implicit *form* and explicit *contents* of *performative contradiction* in which the hypothetical interlocutor operates, namely, the incoherence of the operations with the reports on human discourses and their history. First, the 'deconstruction' of the counter-positions

----

[108]Ibid., pp. 162 and 164 (italics mine). The phrase. "will to knowledge" is Foucault's. On the themes of the death of man and the end of history, see Foucault's *Order of Things: An Archeology of Human Sciences* (New York: Vintage Books, 1970), pp. 367-73, 386-87.

yields to displacement of the naive subject. Secondly, there appears a contradiction between the naïveté or immediacy claimed and the mediating reports communicated by the naive subject. Thirdly, the reversal proceeds from the _interrogation_ of consciousness implicitly operative in the interlocutor's attempts to secure meaning, to _sublation_ of incoherent claims on the truth, reality, objectivity, and the good, to _confinement_, which makes this whole development of meaning explicit.

If the naive realist, materialist, idealist, or the structuralist strives for the _real_ 'out there' or 'in here', _knowing_ by 'taking a good look', _objectivity_ as the 'obviously out there', and the _good_ as in-dwelling in nature to be simply gaped at and acted in an immediate accord with it, then the post-structuralist in the Nietszchean tradition merely rightly confirms that there are no such things as reality, knowing, objectivity, the good, and their history _in the senses defined above_, but only, in Lonergan's words, a catalogue of philosophical nonsense:

> [I]f one agrees with the logical positivists that meaning refers to sensible data or to signs that refer to sensible data, then one must conclude that the majority of philosophers have been indulging in nonsense; it will follow that a history of philosophy is engaged mainly in cataloging and comparing different brands of nonsense; and it will be a matter of small moments just how much nonsense of what brand is attributed to this or that philosopher.[109]

Again:

> If objectivity is a matter of elementary extroversion, then the

---

[109] _Insight_, p. 585.

> objective interpreter has to have more to look at than spatially ordered marks on paper.... But the plain fact is that there is nothing "out there" except spatially ordered marks; to appeal to dictionaries and to grammars, to linguistic and stylistic studies, is to appeal to more marks.... [T]hen there is no objective interpretation whatever; there is only gaping at ordered marks, and the only order is spatial.[110]

If one conceives the counter-positional notions of the real, true, objective, the good, and their histories as normative, then the post-structuralist deconstruction of the human subjectivity, of God, and of history makes only explicit the nihilism operative all along within the above counter-positions. I would contend that this explicitation does not make Derrida, Foucault, Rorty, and others themselves necessarily nihilistic, but rather genuine about the cover-up engendered by the fascination with technique in both the secular and religious brands of nihilism. This cover-up was exposed by Lonergan when he spoke of the logicians as the morticians of technique who try in vain to prevent the decomposition of their systems. Foucault reveals this cover-up in his thematizations of the power-knowledge and bio-power complexes in his studies on the rise of prisons, of medical institutions, or of the phenomena of 'sex' in the oppressive 'pastoral care' of the modern state. The very question of normativity of meaning that informs our common way of life is unmasked in Foucault's work as being embedded in the interstices of technique and power. Hence, his deconstruction signifies not only the end of the previously accepted normative cultural superstructure, but also the abandonment by the post-structuralists of the Western philosophical project for the sake of their practical entry into the interplay of post-modern rationality.

Lonergan's <u>argumentum ad hominem</u> is relevant and

----

[110]Ibid., pp. 582-83.

legitimate in its appeal to both the genuine and truncated sources of the post-modern alternatives: nihilism or relativism--in their two options of madness, as a way to wisdom, and the post-historical totalitarian state--Straussian return to neoclassicism, or the shift to a new stage of meaning through one's self-appropriation of the historical, existential subject.[111]

My concluding remarks will consolidate Lonergan's argument by turning to mediating and mediated phases of the operational development in their convergence of historical consciousness and methodical control of meaning.

E. Conclusion: Convergence of Historical Consciousness and Methodical Control of Meaning

The crisis of historicism led to the crisis of pluralism, but both are crises within the cultural superstructure. The source that gave rise to this crisis of relevant controls of meaning and value can be located within the development of historical consciousness itself, i.e., in: (1) The incredible growth and multiplication of theories; (2) the discovery of a

----

[111]These three alternatives are discussed in Robert Doran's paper "Cosmopolis and the Situation: A Preface to Systematics and Communications" (pp. 17ff of the unpublished conference draft), presented at 1984 Boston College "Lonergan Workshop" as a projected synopsis of his upcoming book. See Robert Doran, "From Psychic Conversion to the Dialectic of Community," in Lonergan Workshop, edited by Fred Lawrence, Vol. 6 (Atlanta, GA: Scholar's Press, 1986), pp. 85-107 Doran traces post-modern philosophical mind-set from the time when Alexandre Kojève delivered his lectures on Hegel's Phenomenology, pb. as Introduction to the Reading of Hegel: Lectures on the Phenomenology of Spirit, translated by James H. Nichols, Jr., edited by Allan Bloom, assembled by Raymond Queneau (Ithaca and London: Cornell University Press, 1980), and he relies on his interpretation on Vincent Descombes, Modern French Philosophy, which I have cited in chap. 1.

historical conditionality of human horizons within the very emergence of historical consciousness, and (3) the breakdown of classicist normativity as the relevant control of meaning.[112]

Nietzsche's and Max Scheler's concerns with *ressentiment*, according to Lonergan, result from an "inflation" of value and meaning long possessed by culture.[113] *Ressentiment* attacks the value quality once had which is now unattainable. *Ressentiment* expresses hatred for the representatives of such lost value quality, and in its hatred, it distorts the whole scale of values. Lewis A. Coser, in his introduction to Scheler's *Ressentiment*, defines the term as "an attitude which arises from a cumulative repression of feelings of hatred, revenge, envy and the like."[114] In Lonergan's analysis, the inferior subject, the neglected, truncated, and immanentist subject, feels not only lack of meaning but also unequal in acquiring the lost quality of common life.[115] Lonergan proposes that the analysis of *ressentiment* can be extended to class, people, epoch, and can "turn out to be a tool of technical, social, and historical criticism."[116] According to Lonergan, what Nietzsche meant by the "death of God," was that atheism, agnosticism, and the 19th century religious indifference destroyed "the meaning of all cultural tradition on which that century was actually living," and, thus, it was necessary to re-create the whole matrix of culture, the whole of history, human self-understanding, memory, and the meaning of informing all of them.[117]

Along with the migration of philosophy away from science, there emerged the celebrated turn to the "neglected subject" (i.e., not treated as such) in classicist thought. If the transposition of the one-dimensional, ahistorical study of the human species in

----

[112]Lamb, *op. cit*., pp. xiii; 358.

[113]Cf. MIT, pp. 33; 273. Cf. Max Scheler, *Ressentiment*, trans. by W.W. Holdheim (New York: Schocken Books, 1961).

[114]Ibid., pp. 23-24.

[115]Cf. *Sub*., in SC, pp. 64ff; also MIT, p. 33.

[116]MIT, p. 33.

[117]TM, p. 39.

terms of the metaphysical soul was long overdue, it has not been successfully completed in the various projects of modernity.[118] Besides the "neglected subject" issuing from the indifference and oversights of classicism, there is also the "truncated subject" who is unaware of the differences between dreaming, waking, and the worlds mediated and constituted by meaning:

> But if universal, daytime somnabulism is not upheld, behaviorists would pay no attention to the inner workings of the subject; logical positivists would confine meaning to sensible data and the structures of mathematical logic; pragmatists would divert our attention to action and results.[119]

While the "truncated subject" condemns itself to an "ahistorical immobilism" and to "an excessively jejune conjunction between abstract concepts and sensible presentations," and so also to one's ignorance of the "proleptic and utterly concrete character of the notion of being"; the "immanentist subject" does not know that one's knowing and doing involve intentional self-transcendence.[120]

The merely immanent subject wants to settle the question of objectivity, being, truth, and the good by picture-thinking. But taking a good look does not release the normative exigencies of intelligence, reasonableness, and responsibility. Since the immanent subject considers judgments to have the same value as intuitions, they can reveal no more than phenomena in the phenomenal world of the immanent subject--these judgments are "a representation of a representation."[121]

----

[118]Cf. Sub., in SC, pp. 69-73.

[119]Ibid., p. 73.

[120]Ibid., pp. 75-6.

[121]Ibid., pp. 77-8; the text cited supra is Lonergan's critical summary of Kantian argument for immanence; on Lonergan's critique of Kant, consult index in Insight, p. 747.

MEDIATION OF DECONSTRUCTION

With the heritage of the 19th century 'deposition' of God and the failure of philosophy to establish a new ground in interiority, and together with the 'extra-scientific opinions' of the scientists and the 'extra-historical opinions' of the historians, the relevance of Lonergan's ad hominem invitation to one's self-appropriation of the operational development of the subject comes as a fundamental option. Again, the argument does not prove that one will find in the subject as subject the radical source of normativity for religious faith, truth, and morality. The argument indicates that in the measure that one does not appropriate one own exigencies for self-transcendence, one will not attain the desired normative meaning and value at all.

Now the problem of historicism and pluralism of ongoing systems poses a limitation of formally systematic control of meaning that would rely on any metaphysical, epistemological, ethical or other theories. For, all systematic objectifications fall prey to ongoing contexts of historicity. Indeed, the limitations formalized in Gödel's theorem, and retrieved by Lonergan in his study of the sciences, lead to the empirical notion of culture; consequently, these limitations make possible a full grasp "of what is meant by a person's historicity."[122]

While 'culture' is a general notion pertaining to the infrastructure of incarnate meaning and value; in superstructure, the empirical notion of culture differs from the normative and universal self-idolatry of the classicist conception of culture. The latter "took its stand on what ought to be, and what ought to be is not to be refuted by what is, "for its bases its hold on reality through its perennial philosophy, immortal works of classics in art and literature, or in the codes of fixed truth.[123] The empirical notion of culture is "culture on the move ... historicist ... man-made ... dynamic."[124] Modern empirical culture is

----

[122]Cf. SC, p. 233.
[123]B in SC, pp. 92-93.
[124]Ibid., p.93.

> a programme of change. It was or is the automatic progress of the liberal, the dialectical materialism of the Marxist, the identification of cosmogenesis and christogenesis by Pierre Teilhard de Chardin. Ours is a time that criticizes and debunks the past, that preaches an ideology, that looks forward to an utopia.[125]

Gödel's limitations express in terms of mathematics the shift from classicism to the empirical notion of culture: "[A]ny set of mathematical definitions and postulates gives rise to further questions that cannot be answered on the basis of definitions and postulates."[126] Lonergan went beyond values and normativity within the world of theory, to an _interrogation_ of mythic and theoretical consciousness on the ground of historical development of meaning. His way of proceeding is from the Socratic _maieutic_ to meta-methodological _maieutic_, in search not of universal definitions, but of methodical control of meaning in terms of the ongoing process of history.[127] As systematic control of meaning was constituted through the differentiation of _logos_ from _mythos_, so methodical exigence promotes the emergence of _methodos_ from _logos_.[128]

Moreover, meta-method converges upon history inasmuch as it results from the historical differentiation of consciousness in the following three stages of culture: mythic, classicist, and modern. The possibility of convergence between historical consciousness and methodical exigence of meaning lies in the _isomorphism_ of the operational development in the ontogenesis of the individual _with_ the development of commons sense, the emergence of theory in fourth

----

[125]Ibid.

[126]_Insights_, chap. XXV.

[127]Robert Doran, _Subject and Psyche: Ricoeur, Jung, and the Search for Foundations_ (Washington, D.C.: University Press of America, 1979), pp. 22-24.

[128]Ibid., p. 24.

century Athens, the discovery of Euclidean geometry with its mathematics of proportions, and further development of the contemporary functional notion of space-time relationships. This isomorphism of the ontogenesis and cultural history of the human species converged in Lonergan's own thinking when his entry into various fields of discourse was linked with his concomitant appropriation of their radical source. Thus, <u>the general notion of mediation is both a result of operational development in the history of ongoing systems and Lonergan's most elementary formulation of methodical control of meaning</u>.

Methodical exigence of the development of meaning unifies the <u>two phases of mediation</u>: the <u>mediating phase</u>, considering the past, and the <u>mediated phase</u> which is oriented to the future. Insofar as method considers the past, the notion of mediation effects the transposition of logical mediation in Aristotle and Hegel (with which I began in Chapter I and comprises functional interrelations of the statistical, classical, and genetic methods of investigation (cf. Fig. 1). In its mediated phase, method includes the dialectical interrogation of the mythic, theoretical, and nihilist positions on reality, truth, objectivity, and the good. Since <u>method involves both a logical and an historical division of operational development</u>, "the notion of mediation has a fundamental meaning insofar as any type of development opens the way to differentiating other worlds."[129]

Inasmuch as method mediates the three basic oppositions in operational development--common sense and theory, the profane and the sacred, exteriority and interiority--so the <u>basic terms</u> and <u>operations</u> denote the self-constituting source of novel developments, and the <u>derived terms</u> and <u>relations</u> include the operational procedures of common sense, of natural and human sciences, of mathematics, of hermeneutics and history, of philosophy and theology. Convergence of historical consciousness and methodical exigence of meaning can be thematized in <u>three senses of mediation</u>: first, the prior development mediates a later development; secondly, a development in one field affects other fields;

----

[129]MoT, pp. 102-106. Consult nn. 5, 36, 75, 80, 81, 85, and 98 to this chapter.

and thirdly, all development mediates the subject as self-constitutive and self-transcending source of possible novel development.

On the one hand, the subject as subject comprises all prior development. Literally, the what of one's nature is mediation (hence implicit definition) of the integral structure of the universe. On the other hand, in the subject as subject, the intelligible yields to intelligent, reasonable, and morally autonomous operational development. As M. Lamb asserts, fresh light is thrown on the <u>mind-and-body problem</u>:

> Both dualism and monism are rejected for the same reason: their confusion of body with thing, of objectivity with extroversion. The correct distinction is not mind-body but intelligent-intelligible; and in man, this proves to be an inadequate distinction since the intelligent is also intelligible, capable of self-analysis.... <u>Intelligence is the escape of intelligibility from the limitations of the empirical residue</u>.[130]

In Lonergan's analysis, the subject as subject is neither a pure transcendental ego standing in opposition to the rest of the reality, nor does the subject as subject vanish through Derrida's deconstructing play of <u>la différance</u>, i.e., through decentering of the intelligent, reasonable, and responsible by the subconscious, senseless, or merely lost in intertextuality. Rather, it is in one's methodical <u>return</u> to elemental meaning in dreams, myth, and common sense; to the transcendental exigence of meaning reaching for God; and to the historicity of the operational development that <u>convergence of historical consciousness with method</u> yields to one's intellectual, moral, and religious conversion. Lonergan's invitation to self-appropriation, rather than being a deconstruction <u>downwards</u>, results in '<u>deconstruction' upwards</u>: "Con-

----

130 Lamb, <u>op. cit</u>. p. 418.

version is the reorganization of the subject, of his operations, of the world with which he is familiar ... [in which] the subject can undergo an upheaval."[131] If the downward shift (e.g. archeology or genealogy) represents an effective denial of the human subject, then the movement upwards is a strategy for the self-affirmation of the human subject. But against the self-affirmation of consciousness that at once is empirical, intellectual, and responsible

> there stands the native bewilderment of the existential subject, revolted by mere animality, unsure of his way through the maze of philosophies, trying to live without a known purpose, suffering despite an unmotivated will, threatened with inevitable death and, before death, with disease and even insanity.[132]

These are not, however, "pure logical alternatives" to the to the reorganization of the subject as subject, for they have their ground in the polymorphic fact of human consciousness (hence the relevant <u>ad hominem</u> character of Lonergan's argumentation), "in the concrete unity-in-tension that is man."[133] Accordingly, the argument cannot be based merely on logical refutation of incoherent intelligence or contradictory methodology, but rather on an <u>ad hominem</u> appeal to one's operational development:

> [I]n the measure that men appropriate their rational self-consciousness, not only do they re-establish the <u>animal rationale</u> but also they break through the phenomenological veil. For . . . they can reach a universal viewpoint from which individual temperament can be discounted, personal evaluations can be criticized, and the

----

[131]MoT, pp. 21-22.
[132]<u>Insight</u>, p. 385.
[133]Ibid.

> many and disparate reports on man, emanating from experts in various fields, can be welded into a single view.[134]

Lonergan's methodical argument, based on one's self-appropriation of the operational development, transcends the limitations of Gödel's theorem by a movement away from merely logical operations to functional mediation of historical development of meaning. When the general notion of mediation is applied to more complex transpositions in a mutual mediation, self-mediation of living, self-mediation of consciousness, conscious mediation by meaning and value, and mediation by self-conscious controls of meaning and value, then the initial theorem of mediation takes on an analogy with what Lonergan calls the scissors-like movement. There is the lower blade of ongoing contexts and provisional categorial specifications, and the upper blade pertaining to 'emergent probability'. Let us consider Lonergan's discussion of the 'upper blade':

> There is an immanent direction in the aggregation of the aggregates in the multicellular formations that is exploited by plants and animals; there is a similar immanent direction exercised by the censorship over contents to emerge into consciousness; and so, in the limiting case of man, the intelligible yields to the intelligent, and the higher system is replaced by a perennial source of higher systems.[135]

Again, the notion of mediation is applied as itself a transcendental function to Gödel's limitations:

> Let us say that this noetic activity is engaged in a lower context [of the scissors-like move-

----

[134] OPI, p. 6.
[135] Insight, p. 269 (italics mine).

> ment] when it is doing mathematics or following scientific method or exercising common sense. Then it will be moving towards an upper context when it scrutinizes mathematics or science or common sense in order to grasp the nature of noetic activity ... it can be shown that the upper context is invariant, that any attempt to revise it <u>can be legitimate only if the hypothetical reviser refutes his own attempt by invoking experience, understanding, and reflection</u>....[136]

The hypothetical reviser, relativist, or nihilist might reject Lonergan's approach as an irrelevant, <u>ad hominem</u> argument. But such a refusal, Lonergan replies, can be legitimate only by appealing, <u>ad hominem</u>. The legitimacy of <u>ad hominem</u> in a philosophical dialogue issues from discrepancies between the relativist's claim and performance. Unless one wants to remain silent, one has to appeal to experience, understanding, judgment, and one's communication thereof in order to deny the import of experience, intelligence, reasonableness, and intelligent community of discourse. Lonergan calls this an impossibility of revision:

> Clearly, revision cannot revise its own presuppositions. A reviser cannot appeal to data to deny data, to his new insights to deny insights, to his new formulation to deny formulation, to his reflective grasp to deny reflective grasp.[137]

This discrepancy or <u>performative contradiction</u> is <u>relevant</u> to the argument; hence the very meaning of <u>ad hominem</u> as the fallacy of irrelevance (a handy tool of the mortician) is a form of cover-up, or a counter-position, subject to deconstruction. The cover-up consists in calling irrelevant what in fact is the only relevant base in genuine philosophic argumentation:

----

[136]Ibid., p. xxvi (italics mine).
[137]Ibid., p. 336.

human experience, understanding, judgment, deliberation, and their self-mediating, operational development. The problem of relativism, or its varieties in nihilism, positivism, and naive realism, arises not because of the neglect of the lower blade in discourse, but the lack of the appropriate upper blade.[138] First, if the lower blade comprises correlations, hypotheses, experiments, and revisions of the hypotheses; the upper blade of methodical mediation is a dynamic heuristic structure of the universe:

> [T]he nature to be known will be expressed by some function; this function will satisfy differential equations that can be reached from quite general considerations; moreover, the function will satisfy a canon of invariance and, in the case of full abstraction from observers, a canon of equivalence as well.[139]

Secondly, in terms of mediation by meaning:

> For the [potential] totality of meanings the upper blade is the assertion that the protean notion of being is differentiated by a series of genetically and dialectically related unknowns. For the [potential] totality of modes of expression the upper blade is the assertion that there is a genetic process in which modes of expression move towards their specialization and differentiation on sharply distinguishable levels.[140]

Thirdly, human nature, when conceived methodically, will comprise its mediating phase of one's historicity and mediated phase of intentional functions

----

[138]Ibid., p. 578.
[139]Ibid., p. 577.
[140]Ibid., p. 578.

satisfying the 'differential equation' of notional, transcendental imperatives: be attentive, be intelligent, be reasonable, be responsible, acknowledge your historicity, be in love!

In neither of the above cases of the upper blade of methodical mediation is 'method' to be conceived as a technique, as, for example, in the New Method Laundry. While a technique might satisfy the relativist or help to cover-up the performative contradictoriness of the nihilist, it does not satisfy the upper blade of the transcendental notions; for these notions not only promote one's self-transcendence, but also provide the criteria of genuineness and freedom. Thus, any technique is subject not only to its own decomposition, but also to a 'deconstructive' movement of the scissors-like mediation by methodical exigence of meaning.

The dialectical method completes the tree of methodical mediation by reversing both the three counter-positional sources of the classcist *philosophia perennis*--materialism, idealism, and naive realism--and the post-modern dissolution of the subject, of history, and of religious faith.[141] For the sake of methodical mediation of meaning, Lonergan distinguishes five worlds we live in: the world of immediacy, the world mediated and constituted by meaning, the world controlled by theory, the world of interiority, and the world oriented to transcendent mystery. He has argued that these worlds do not group together, but rather represent three distinct stages in culture or three ways meaning mediates our reality.

Now when the limitations in grouping are not adverted to, there can result a number of confusions. "The naive realist" knows the world mediated by meaning, but says that it is by "taking a good look" out-there-now that the real, the true, the objective, and the good are attained. The "naive idealist" holds that "to be is to perceive or to be perceived."[142] But to be pertains to the world mediated and constituted by meaning, whereas the "perceived" is the given in the

----

[141]CAM, p. 152.
[142]Cf. MIT, pp. 263-64.

world of immediacy. The "die-hard empiricist" "eliminates from the world mediated by meaning everything that is not given in the world of immediacy."[143] "The critical idealist" enacts the long overdue Copernican turn to the subject but only further confesses the matter:

> He [e.g., Kant] combines the operations of understanding and reason, not with data of sense, but with sensitive intuitions of phenomena, where the phenomena are the appearing, if not of nothing, then of things themselves, which while unknowable, manage to get talked about through the device of limiting concept.[144]

"The absolute idealist" explores the depth of meaning, refutes naive realists, but does not advance to the critical exigence of meaning. In all five positions above, knowing is some single operation rather than a whole dynamic cognitional structure (experience, understanding, judgment, deliberation). For example, objectivity, for the naive realist, is not a combination of distinct properties in distinct operations, but a single property of looking, sensing, intuiting, perceiving, etc. But

> the objectivity of intellectual operations is not similar to the objectivity of sensitive operations, and ... to demand similarity as an _a priori_ condition of the possibility of objective intellectual operations is to demand that rational psychology be reduced to a _terra incognita_.[145]

The relation of the intellectual operations to those of sense is not their similarity, but "functional

---

[143]Ibid., p. 264.
[144]CS, in _Coll._, p. 235.
[145]CS, in _Coll._, p. 235.

complementarity"; in the same manner, their objectivity does not reside in their resemblance to the ocular vision, but "because they are what ocular vision never is, namely, intelligent and rational."[146] Both the idealist and naive realist are embedded in a 'picture world' bound by their 'picture thinking', by knowing as looking, by Anschauung as the immediate relation of cognition to objects, and by their "forgetfulness of being."[147]

Reacting to these confusions, Kierkegaard moves away from logic, since life, movement, and freedom of concrete human existence cannot be inserted into a logic (only their Idea can). Lonergan points out that Kierkegaard marks a trend in a subsequent development in philosophy: Where Kierkegaard stressed religious faith, Nietzsche was concerned with power, Dilthey turned to concrete human living, Husserl analyzed the constitution of our intending, Bergson talked about élan vital, Blondel specified action, American pragmatists studied results, and European existentialists were preoccupied with authentic subjectivity.[148]

Lonergan concludes that these contemporary trends did not effect clarification but only a shift in the meanings of "objective" and "subjective," and that disagreements as to the meaning of those terms are due "to the subjectivity of philosophers, moralists, religious people."[149] While Karl Jaspers would admit that one's self-appropriation elucidates the subject's own meaning--whether good or evil--he would not consider it to be an objective knowledge.[150] The context of all these contemporary trends will not be resolved, Lonergan says, until the ambiguities of the three sources of the philosophia perennis--materialism, realism, and idealism in all their variations--are overthrown. This resolution is what I named Lonergan's project of 'deconstruction' and juxtaposed it to Derrida's original meaning of deconstruction:

----

[146]Ibid.

[147]Ibid., p. 236; on Kant, see reference in n. 2 there.

[148]MIT, p. 264.

[149]Ibid., p. 265.

[150]Ibid., pp. 263; 265.

> From the welter of conflicting philosophic definitions, and from the Babel of endless philosophic arguments, it has been concluded that the object of philosophy either does not exist or cannot be attained. But this conclusion disregards two facts. On the one hand, the philosophers have been men of exceptional acumen and profundity. On the other hand, the many, contradictory, disparate philosophies can all be clarification of some basic but polymorphic fact; because the fact is basic, its implications range over the universe; but because it is polymorphic, its alternative forms ground diverse sets of implications.... In the light of the dialectic, then, the historical series of philosophies would be regarded as a sequence of contributions to a single but complex goal.... However, the dialectic itself has a notable presupposition, for it supposes that cognitional theory exercises a fundamental influence in metaphysics, in ethics, and in theological pronouncements.[151]

The resolution, then, offered in Lonergan's methodical analysis of operational development consists in mediation of the worlds of immediacy and mediation by authentic subjectivity. When the worlds of common sense and of theory are mediated by interiority, then one can distinguish between object and objectivity in either of those worlds. Further, mediation and methodical exigence of meaning and value can move from one world to another without trying to form a single, homogeneous, monolythic group, i.e., without totalizing ambitions of distinct horizons over the rest of them.[152]

----

[151]Insight, pp. 386-7; 389.

Finally, using Nietzsche's expression and "transvaluing it," transcendental exigence of meaning promotes the human subject to religious experience which trans-values all values.[153]

It is in the realm of the transcendental exigence of meaning that God's gift of love emerges as a distinct world of meaning. It is in this existential realm that the "deliberate shift of center"[154] of the subject as subject mediates the mystic's return from the worlds of common sense, myth, theory, and "the other interiority into a 'cloud of unknowing,'' in order to live in those worlds with greater intensity of faith.[155]

Retracing the development from the religious pattern of experience, through the infrastructure of intersubjectivity, to transcendental control of meaning, it is clear that what holds for human intersubjectivity is also true of the immediate relationship between human beings and God. There is the word of God that enters our immediacy prior to its thematizations in art, symbols, language, theologies, and cultures - its carrier may be human intersubjectivity.[156] "Before it enters the world mediated by meaning, religion is the prior word God speaks to us by flooding our hearts with his love."[157] That prior word, just as the self-constitutive function of consciousness, is communicated in a world of immediacy, and "to the unmediated experience of the mystery of love and awe."[158] That prior word of God is "a vector, an undertow, a fateful call to a dreaded holiness."[159] That prior word of God, "the fact that God's love has flooded our inmost hearts through the Holy Spirit he has given us," is also "the real root and ground of unity...."[160]

----

[152]TM, p. 48.
[153]SC, introduction, p. 3.
[154]Cf. MCP.
[155]MIT, p. 266 (italics mine).
[156]Ibid., p. 112.
[157]Ibid.
[158]Ibid.; note the difference between mythic consciousness and mystic's openness to the Divine mystery.
[159]Ibid., p. 113.

On the other hand, the mystic's withdrawal from the world mediated by the "constructs of culture and the whole complicated mass of mediating operations" is "a new, mediated immediacy of his subjectivity reaching for God."[161] The difference between the prior word of God in our empirical self-presence and the second, mediated return to immediacy by deliberately chosen solitude of the mystic, consists, then, in the undifferentiated infrastructure of consciousness and the differentiated functions and controls of meaning in religious cultural superstructure.

The difference, then, is between the infrastructure of the religious pattern of experience and the superstructure of the transcendental exigence of meaning. The former exhibits the mankind's thrust and orientation towards the mystery, the known unknown.[162] As Lamb points out:

> [E]ven the experience of atheism, of absurdity and nausea, bear witness to this religious dimension. For, if there was not any ultimate meaning, value and goodness somehow present within the conscious depth of man, how could he possibly experience nausea and absurdity?[163]

Human thrust towards the known unknown of the mystery is marked by the dilemma of the subject as it exists in that prior, ontological freedom of the patterned conscious self-presence, and the freedom of the intelligent, rational, and responsible subject who con-

----

[160]Ibid., p. 327; reference made by Lonergan is to the Romans 5,5.

[161]Ibid., p. 29 (italics mine): reference made by Lonergan to Insight, pp. 181 ff. See other examples and references on peak experience and mystical experience in MIT, n. 1, p. 29.

[162]Insight, pp. 531-34; 639-44; cf. NE, p. 20.

[163]Lamb, op. cit., p. 267. On absurdity, the death of God and of the subject, See Lonergan's Sub., in SC, p. 86.

stitutes itself "in light of better knowledge and with a full responsibility."[164] The drama of the self-constituting subject cannot be escaped by some refusal to "remake ourselves...for that is just assuming responsibility for whatever we happen inadvertently to have made ourselves in the past."[165]

Historically, the differences between both the East and the South and the secular West reside in their principal differentiation of consciousness relating the basic developmental oppositions as those of common sense and transcendence (in the East and the South) and common sense and theory (in the West); whereas the predominant differentiation and opposition in the historical development of meaning in the East, the South, and the Christian West is between common sense and transcendence.[166] Thus, it is the theoretical differentiation of consciousness that separates the Western development of meaning from the East and the South, and the crisis of both theoretical and critical controls of meaning in the West that causes the East and the Third World in general to seek alternatives to the Western inculturation of religious hope.

The transpositions and the crisis of meaning in contemporary Western culture, including Communist Central and Eastern Europe, and the growing domination of technique in place of theoretical and critical controls of meaning in the Third World, account for decline of mutual self-mediation among these societies and for all sorts of oppression by totalizing horizons. Any totalizing horizon can become politically and economically totalitarian, and various controls of meaning can fall prey to the interstices of power. The Soviet and the Western worlds are informed by their common roots in modern development, transpositions, and decline of meaning; moreover, both share this contemporary decline with Christian churches. The totalitarian temptation to dominate entices all three to embalm the decomposition of their biases in a mortician-like denial of the mortality of technique. Lonergan's work was to face this temptation, without a

---

[164]NE, p. 24.
[165]Ibid.
[166]MIT, p. 266.

resort to a utopia, but nevertheless through genuine hope in human development mediated by "God's love flooding our inmost hearts through the Holy Spirit he has given us...."[167]

I conclude with Lonergan's own written words read at the funeral mass of the Resurrection, in Toronto, on the 29th of November, 1984, as an epitaph to his life struggle:

> As the question of God is implicit in all our questioning, so being in love with God is the basic fulfillment of our conscious intentionality. That fulfillment brings a deep-set joy that can remain despite humiliation, failure, privation, pain, betrayal, desertion.... [It] bears fruit in a love of one's neighbour.... [T]he absence of that fulfillment opens the way ... to the harshness of human life arising from the ruthless exercise of power, to despair about human welfare springing from the conviction that the universe is absurd.[168]

----

[167]Romans 5, 5.
[168]MIT, p. 105.

EPILOGUE

FROM SUSPICION TO RECOVERY: MEDIATION OF EDUCATION FOR LIBERATION

The power of methodical analysis is indicated by the brevity of the initial theorem of mediation and by the possibilities of its further complication. While Lonergan's formulation is easy to grasp in the case of the general mediation of the watch, perhaps more difficult in the case of the functional whole of a mutual mediation, and quite complex in describing genetic method and operational development; its application to one's self-appropriation of that self-conscious operational development, within all the carriers of incarnate meaning in cultural infrastructure and on all four levels of intentional self-presence, may lead "to an upheaval of the subject."

This upheaval of the subject corresponds to what Paul Ricoeur defined as a movement of critique and suspicion represented by the 19th century "masters of suspicion"[1] (Nietzsche, Marx, and Freud) and their 20th century counterparts (Derrida, Foucault, Lacan *et al.*); while a self-appropriation of human conscious operational development (mediating and mediated phases of methodical analysis) parallels the movement towards the restoration of critical reason represented by the 20th century masters of recovery (Habermas, Lonergan, Ricoeur). These two movements in their suspicion (of

----

[1]Paul Ricoeur, *Freud and Philosophy*, trans. Denis Savage (New Haven: Yale University Press, 1980), pp. 32-36, 459-93. On the link among phenomenology, critical theory, Lonergan's methodology, and the themes of suspicion and recovery vis-à-vis the project of the Enlightenment, consult James L. Marsh, "Dialectical Phenomenology: From Suspension to Suspicion" in *Man and World* 17 (Netherlands: Martinus Nijhoff Publishers, 1984), pp. 121-141; "Heidegger's Overcoming of Metaphysics: A Critique" *Journal of the British Society for Phenomenology* Vol. 16 No. 1 (January 1985), pp. 55-69.

human subjectivity, of human history, and of God) and recovery of human subjectivity, of history (Habermas, Lonergan, Ricoeur) and of God (Lonergan, Ricoeur) are integrated within Lonergan's method in philosophy, namely as a dialectical movement of mediation of education for liberation.

The dialectical movement of mediation of education for liberation is thus the integration of the upheaval, decentering, reorganization, or suspicion of the historical subject and of what Lonergan calls one's intellectual, moral, and religious conversion. The two phases of this dialectical movement (this movement reverses the counter-positions on reality, truth, objectivity, and the good as these are found in the history of ideas and in the practices within different cultures and disciplines--see figure 1.) are homological but not identical with Plato's similes of one's conversion to the Good in the stories of the Cave and the Divided Line in the Republic. Though the notion of reorganization of the subject through 'deconstruction', sublation, and self-mediation depends on differentiation of the basic set of functional interrelations which I discussed in Chapter 1, operational development aiming at these conversions in question does not directly correspond to historical development from the traditional, to the classicist, modern, and contemporary stages of culture.[2] If Lonergan's notion of mediation may be depicted as his transposition of the themes of liberal arts education in Plato, of conversion in Plato and St. Augustine, of the field of both the Aristotelian and Hegelian logic, and of their philosophy of nature, into a form of implicit definition patterned according to the theorem of mediation in general (Part One of this study), then his thematization of self-mediation in human operational development is his transposition of both the Hegelian-Marxist and of the contemporary classical and critical phenomenology (Part Two of this study). In both cases these transformations converge upon concrete, i.e. existential human subjects: the subject as subject of consciousness, the subject as rational knower, the subject as responsible doer, the subject as historically self-

----

[2]On basic and derived general categories, see Lonergan's excellent summary in MIT, pp. 285-88.

conscious, and subject as lover of the Divine. Consciousness is not another operation or perception to be added to the set of basic operations, or proved from without, but is the prior prerequisite for any self-mediation by meaning and value. Likewise, intellectual, moral, and religious conversions cannot be imagined, nor do they undergo development isomorphic to the general pattern of mediation, but rather conversions are the prior prerequisite of the novel stage of development for which our present time calls. In brief, conversions complete the set of displacements that complement the set of isomorphisms of mediation--the displacement upwards, inwards, and the deliberate shift of center. Conversions make a higher level of self-mediation possible; and with them also emerges a possibility of a novel stage of cultural superstructure; indeed, they are the necessary prerequisites for our contemporary, global life-world to survive at all.

Lonergan has spent many years developing methodical analysis, and he ventured into many fields of human discourse. But his chief concern in developing method was the need to mount to the level of our time, the need for authentic self-knowledge, if we are to go on as a civilization. Modernity has generated a new sense of autonomy, for we are a culture that knows about itself and other cultures.[3] Our culture is aware of its human origins and of the individual and collective responsibility for the world we live in, the one which we have constituted by meaning and motivated by value. Nevertheless,

> concern for the future, if it is not just high-sounding hypocrisy, supposes rare moral attainment ... not indeed in the sense that the past is to be restored, but in the sense that our creativity has to discover the future and our determination has to realize it.[4]

The extent and complexity of modern specializa-

---

[3]GMC, in SC, p. 115.
[4]Ibid., p. 116.

tions preclude the possibility in our age of Renaissance universal knowledge, or of the medieval author of the _Summa_,

> we know too much in too many fields; we have witnessed too much suffering in too many unexpected quarters, to purchase confidence by an easy exuberance of feeling or to accept words of assurance without answers to our questions.[5]

Lonergan's argument, then, is concerned _with the conditions preliminary to an effective collaboration_:

> For in the measure that potential collaborators move towards a personal appropriation of their own rational self-consciousness ... will they begin to attain the needed common vision of the common goal. In the measure that they discover in themselves the structure of developing intelligence ... will they share a tentative idea that can unify and coordinate separate efforts in different fields. In the measure, again, that they reach the invariants of intellectual development ... will they possess a central nucleus that retains its identity through all the possible developments of human intelligence.[6]

The legitimacy and the relevance of Lonergan's argument and his invitation to one's self-appropriation of that creative source of development can at best be experienced, understood, judged, and deliberated about in a genuine dialectical movement from suspicion to recovery, i.e. in the dialectic of 'deconstruction', sublation, and mediation. Such a movement, thematized

----

[5]OPI, p. 5.
[6]Ibid., p. 6.

concretely and existentially through an ongoing collaboration of inquirers (students, professors, scholars, scientists, philosophers, and theologians, et al.) would provide a contemporary context of education for liberation of the whole person and of cosmopolis. Even though such "system on the move" does not exist, and even though we know and, at times, despair about the breakdown of the old and the impasse of the present, we have no other option than to promote a suspicion of all bias and to seek healing and recovery of human creativity.[7]

In what follows, I wish to offer a formal sketch of how Lonergan's methodology could be concretely developed in an ongoing, collaborative mediation of education for liberation. In my example I will have in mind a hypothetical undergraduate course in philosophy of human nature, ethics, or intellectual history.

Mediation of education for liberation would have three components of a concrete, existential syllogism (Figure 8.):

I. THE PRIMARY TEXT are the invariants of the subject as subject, i.e. the student and his or her ordinary sequence of learning activities (operations).

II. SECONDARY TEXTS are variables predicated of

---

[7]See Bernard Lonergan, "Healing and Creating in History" in A Third Collection: Papers by Bernard Lonergan, S.J. Edited by Frederick E. Crowe, S.J. (New York: Paulist Press, 1985).

On an attempt at creating a contemporary, ongoing and collaboratory context of education for liberation, consult Core Studies Program: Core Curriculum Committee Report No.3 (Los Angeles: Loyola Marymount University, January 1987). This is presently the only known proposal for a revision of the core studies at a North American University which explicitly utilizes Lonergan's methodology in specifying an integrating idea of education in terms of human operational development.

the subject as subject: (A) COMMENTARIES of other thinkers, of the history of ideas, of theories, and of various world-views about human development; (B) COMMENTARIES by other students, professors, or guest speakers in an ongoing collaboration of inquirers, i.e. their formulation of ideas, theories, world-views, development, and living.

I.	THE PRIMARY TEXT [The student]
II.	SECONDARY TEXTS [Commentaries: books and others]
III.	SELF-APPROPRIATION of one's HUMAN OPERATIONAL DEVELOPMENT [Intellectual moral, and religious conversion; transcendental precepts; collaboration]

Figure 8. Mediation of education for liberation

III. SELF-APPROPRIATION of the PRIMARY TEXT, of one's human operational development, will comprise what Lonergan calls (1) the minimum core requirement, namely intellectual, moral, and religious conversion of the operating human subject:

> By religious conversion, which is the foundation of the other two, I mean the habitual acceptance of God's gift of his love flooding our hearts through the Holy Spirit he has given us (Rom. 5,5). By moral conversion I mean the existential decision to guide one's decisions and one's actions not by satisfactions but by values, by what truly is worth while. By intellectual conversion I mean an adequate understanding of the difference between the world of immediacy (in which the infant lives) and the world mediated by meaning and motivated by value (into which the child, the adolescent, the adult gradually enter).... Such conversions involve radical shifts of horizon....

and (2) the two distinct modes of human development, namely ontogenesis and history:

> [Human development] moves from below upwards inasmuch as it begins from one's personal experience, advances through ever fuller understanding and more balanced judgment, and so attains the responsible exercise of personal freedom.
>
> It moves from above downwards inasmuch as one belongs to a hierarchy of groups and so owes allegiance to one's home, to one's country, to one's religion. Through the traditions of the group one is socialized, acculturated, educated to become in time either (1) a member of the tribe or clan or (2) an inheritor of the classicism of ancient Greece and Rome or (3) a participant in the modernity that is familiar with the variety of human cultures and literatures, the achievements of modern mathematics and science, the expertise of the contemporary exegete and historian, the reflections of philosophers and theologians.
>
> These two modes of development are interdependent. Both begin from infancy. But only through the second does the first take one beyond the earliest prehistoric stages of human development. Only through the first is there any real assimilation and appropriation of the second.[8]

----

[8]Bernard Lonergan, "Questionnaire on Philosophy" [1976] Method: Journal of Lonergan Studies Vol. 2, No. 2 (Oct 1984), pp. 11-12; 10. [Hereafter abbreviated as QP.] On the two modes of human

The two modes of human development include then the invariants of human ontogenesis and the variables of human history, community and of the contents of historical consciousness represented by individuals and groups within modern cultures:

[Invariants]	HUMAN DEVELOPMENT: ONTOGENESIS
WORLD-VIEW/	LEARNING OPERATIONS IN ORDINARY SEQUENCE
IMMEDIACY/	EMPIRICAL level/ EXPERIENCE
[sensing, perceiving, creative and representative imagining, remembering, feeling]	
MEDIATED and EFFECTED by meaning/	INTELLECTUAL and INTERPRETATIVE level/ UNDERSTANDING
[questioning, inquiring, conceiving, formulating]	
	RATIONAL and REFLECTIVE level/ JUDGMENT
[reflection, marshalling and weighing evidence]	
CONSTITUTED by meaning and value	RESPONSIBLE level/ DELIBERATION
[evaluation, moral judgment, decision-making, acting]	

Figure 9. THE PRIMARY TEXT: Invariants of learning operations in their ordinary sequence.

[Variables]	HUMAN DEVELOPMENT: HISTORY of CULTURES
WORLD-VIEW/	CONTROLS OF MEANING AND VALUE IN HISTORICAL SEQUENCE OF BASIC OPPOSITIONS
	UNDIFFERENTIATED CONTROLS
MYTHIC/	TRADITIONAL mediation/ COMMON SENSE meanings
	DIFFERENTIATED CONTROLS
	TRANSCENDENTAL control/ PROFANE-SACRED
CLASSICAL/	THEORETICAL control/ COMMON SENSE-THEORY
MODERN/	CRITICAL control/ EXTERIORITY-INTERIORITY
CONTEMPORARY/	METHODICAL cont./ FUNCTIONAL SPECIALTIES

Figure 10. SECONDARY TEXTS: Variables of commentaries, history of ideas, cultural development, world-views.

----

development, consult Lonergan's HCH, in TC, pp. 100-109.

FROM SUSPICION TO RECOVERY: MEDIATION OF EDUCATION FOR LIBERATION

The meaning of the expression "mediation of education for liberation" lies then in the dialectical interplay between the subject and the predicate, i.e. human development in ontogenesis and in history of cultures. As ontogenesis reaches its peak in the constitutive functions of meaning, the responsible and deliberative operations of the agent, so also the development of cultures (birth, growth, decline, renaissance, breakdown) is marked off by the stages in the control of meaning. To appropriate the invariants of human development is to understand history of cultures, one's own historicity, oneself and one's community as the source of novel development. Thus, education which mediates the possibility of contemporary culture to not only understand its past but to appropriate the dynamic foundations of its ongoing creativity is an education for liberation.

The outcome of mediation and thematization of the twofold movement of human development specifies the meaning of self-appropriation, namely (A) TRANSCENDENTAL PRECEPTS and (B) CONVERSIONS:

TRANSCENDENTAL PRECEPTS	
(1) BE ATTENTIVE AND SENSITIVE!	
(2) BE INTELLIGENT!	
(3) BE REFLECTIVE AND REASONABLE!	
(4) BE RESPONSIBLE AND LOVING!	
(5) ACKNOWLEDGE YOUR HISTORICITY!	
CONVERSIONS	
INTELLECTUAL	[Differentiate between the foundations of the worlds of immediacy and those mediated by meaning and value!
MORAL	[Differentiate between the foundations of choices in satisfaction and in existential appropriation of values!]
RELIGIOUS	[Mediate God's love spoken to immediacy of our consciousness by your habitual acceptance, i.e. prayer!]

Figure 11. SELF-APPROPRIATION OF HUMAN DEVELOPMENT.

It is a student's self-appropriation of human operational development--mediated by secondary texts of the course content, of the professor's contribution, and of interaction with the community of inquirers--which is the intended goal of the core program in the liberal arts education. It is a student's use of transcendental precepts--in light of intellectual, moral, and religious conversion--which is the method within the specialized fields or functional specialties of learning.

Finally, an example of a possible syllabus in a core program that would advert to Lonergan's method in philosophy, while not necessarily becoming a course on "Lonergan's philosophy," would have to follow the two modes of human development: (1) The ordinary sequence of learning operational activities, (2) historical sequence of differentiated controls of meaning and value, while (3) preparing ground for this methodology in the prologue and mediating the intended goal in the epilogue to the course. While the invariants of human development are not revisable, the variables of secondary texts offer numerous possibilities in structuring the particular courses and choosing the texts:

DIVISION OF THE COURSE	[FOCUS/CONTENT]	[EXAMPLE]
PROLOGUE:	Human development/ mediation	[Lonergan, "Dimensions of Meaning"]
FROM TRADITION TO CLASSICAL JUDEO-CHRISTIAN WORLD-VIEW:	The rise of theoretical control of meaning	[Homer, Plato, Aristotle, Augustine, Cicero, Aquinas]
FROM CLASSICISM TO MODERNITY:	The shift to interiority	[Descartes, Galileo, Locke, Hume, Kant, Hegel]
FROM THE CRISIS OF MODERNITY TO CONTEMPORARY INTER-DISCIPLINARY WORLD-VIEW:	crisis of modernity and the search for method	[Nietzsche, Marx, Freud, Kierkegaard, Dostoevsky, Camus, Sartre, Husserl, Habermas, Ricoeur, Becker, Lonergan]
EPILOGUE:	Self-appropriation of human development/ thematization of mediation and of method	[Lonergan, "Healing and Creating in History"]

Figure 12. A sample syllabus of the core program of mediation of education for liberation.

Thus while the variables of human history provide the material for the moment of suspicion, the invariants of human ontogenesis are the foundation of the possibility of suspicion. Self-appropriation of the human core and methodical mediation of human discourses are an ongoing human journey from suspicion to recovery.

BIBLIOGRAPHY

PRIMARY SOURCES

A. Published Works by Bernard J. F. Lonergan, S.J.

Bernard Lonergan: 3 Lectures. Edited by R. Eric O'Connor. Montreal: Thomas More Institute, 1975.

Caring about Meaning: Patterns in the life of Bernard Lonergan. Edited by Pierrot Lambert, Charlotte Tansey, Cathleen Going. Montreal, Canada: Thomas More Institute, 1982.

Collection: Papers by Bernard Lonergan, S.J. Edited and with an Introduction by Fred E. Crowe, S.J. London: Darton, Longman & Todd, and New York: Herder & Herder, 1967.

Doctrinal Pluralism. Milwaukee: Marquette University Press, 1971.

Insight: A Study of Human Understanding. New York: Philosophical Library, and London: Longmans, Green & Company, 1957.

"The Mediation of Christ in Prayer." Method: Journal of Lonergan Studies. Vol. 2, No. 1 (March 1984): 1-20.

"Merging Horizons: System, Common Sense, Scholarship," Cultural Hermeneutics 7 (1973): 87-99.

Method in Theology. New York: Herder & Herder, Inc., 1972.

"The Original Preface fo Insight," Method: Journal of Lonergan Studies Vol. 3 No. 1 (March 1985): 3-7.

Philosophy of God, and Theology. Philadelphia: The Westminster Press, 1973.

"Questionnaire on Philosophy," _Method: Journal of Lonergan Studies_ Vol. 2 No. 2 (Oct 1984): 1-35.

"Religious Experience." Edited by Thomas A. Dunne and Jean-Marc Laporte. _Trinification of the World_. Toronto: Regis College Press, 1978: 71-83.

A Second Collection: Papers by Bernard Lonergan, S.J. Edited, with an Introduction by William F. J. Ryan, S.J. and Bernard J. Tyrrell, S.J. London: Darton, Longman & Todd, and Philadelphia: The Westminster Press, 1974.

A Third Collection: Papers by Bernard Lonergan, S.J. Edited by Frederick E. Crowe, S.J. New York: Paulist Press, 1985.

Understanding and Being: An Introduction and Companion to Insight. The Halifax Lectures by Bernard Lonergan. Edited by Elizabeth and Mark Morelli. New York: The Edwin Mellen Press, 1980.

Verbum: Word and Idea in Aquinas. Edited by David Burrell, C.S. Notre Dame: University of Notre Dame Press, 1967.

B. Unpublished manuscripts, lectures, notes, drafts, outlines, and transcripts from tapes by Bernard J. F. Lonergan, S.J.

[The following documents are available from the Canadian Lonergan Institute at Regis College, Toronto; from the North American Lonergan Centers at The University of Santa Clara, Boston College; and similar international centers in Italy, Ireland, West Germany, Philippines, and Australia.]

"The Analogy of Meaning." Edited by Philip McShane. Regis College, Toronto, April 1973. A typescript of a lecture delivered on September 28, 1963 at Thomas More Institute.

"Critical Realism and the Integration of the Sciences." Dublin: University College, May 23-25, 1961. Six lectures on Insight given in Dublin, and an Appendix with a summary of question-answer period.

De methodo theologiae, notae desumptae ab alumnis. [On Method In Theology, notes distributed to students.] Rome, Italy: The Gregorian University, 1962.

An Essay in Circulation Analysis. Boston: Boston College, 1944, 1978, 1980, 1982. A typewritten manuscript of Lonergan's early draft and later revisions of his macroeconomic analysis.

"Lectures on Mathematical Logic." Boston: Boston College, 1957. Mimeographed class notes.

"Mediation." Gonzaga: Spokane, 1963. The outline and summary of Lonergan's lecture now published as "The Mediation of Christ in Prayer."

"Meaning as a Category for Interpretation." Washington, D. C.: The Catholic University of America, April 25-26, 1969. A transcript from a private tape-recording.

"Method of Theology." Toronto: Regis College, 1962. A transcript from a recording of Lonergan's summer institute.

"Notes on Existentialism." Boston: Boston College, 1957. Mimeographed class notes.

On the Ontological and Psychological Constitution of Christ. Translated by Timothy Fallon, S.J. Rome: Gregorian University, 1956, 1957, 1958. A book-length manuscript is available from T. Fallon, Philosophy Department of the University of Santa Clara.

Philosophy of Education. Cincinnati, Ohio: Xavier College, 1959. A book-length manuscript of Lonergan's lectures.

"(Towards) a Definition of Education." February 9, 1949. Private notes by Bernard Lonergan. (Typewritten.)

"What is Claude-Lévi Strauss up to?" Toronto: Regis College, 1978). A typewritten paper for the Toronto conference on hermeneutics and structuralism.

SECONDARY SOURCES

[The secondary sources cited by Lonergan and mentioned in this study are marked with an asterisk.]

Books

Altizer, J. J. Thomas, _et al_. _Deconstruction and Theology_. New York: Crossroad, 1982.

Arato, Andrew and Gebhardt, Eike (Editors). Introduction by Paul Piccone. _The Essential FRANKFURT SCHOOL Reader_. New York: Continuum, 1985.

Aristotle. _The Basic Works of Aristotle_. Edited by Richard McKeon. New York: Random House, 1941.*

Atkins, Douglas G. _Reading Deconstruction: Deconstructive Reading_. Kentucky: The University Press of Kentucky, 1983.

Bernstein, Richard J. (Editor). _Habermas and Modernity_. Cambridge, Massachusets: The MIT Press, 1985.

______. _Philosophical Profiles: Essays in Pragmatic Mode_. Philadelphia: University of Pennsylvania Press, 1986.

Binswanger, Ludwig. _Le rêve et l'existence_. Translation and 130-pages long Preface by Michel Foucault. Paris: Desclee, 1954.*

Cassirer, Ernst. _The Philosophy of Symbolic Forms_. Vols. I-III. Translated by Ralph Menheim. New Haven: Yale University Press, 1953, 1955, 1957.*

Core Studies Program: Core Curriculum Committee Report No.3 (Los Angeles: Loyola Marymount University, January 1987). Issued for internal use only.

Derrida, Jacques. Dissemination. Translated, and with an Introduction and notes, by Barbara Johnson. Chicago: University of Chicago Press, 1981.

______. Of Grammatology. Translated by Gayatri Chakravorty Spivak. Baltimore: John Hopkins University Press, 1976.

______. Positions. Translated by Alan Bass. London: Athlone Press, 1981.

______. Speech and Phenomena: And Others Essays on Husserl's Theory of Signs. Translated by David B. Allisom. Evanston, Illinois: Northwestern University Press, 1973.

______. Writing and Difference. Translated by Alan Bass. London: Routledge and Kegan Paul, 1978.

Descombes, Vincent. Modern French Philosophy. Translated by L. Scott-Fox and J. M. Harding. Cambridge: Cambridge University Press, 1980.

Doran, Robert M. Subject, and Psyche: Ricoeur, Jung, and the search for Foundations. Washington, D.C.: University Press of America, 1979.

Einstein, Albert. Essays in Science. New York: Philosophical Library, 1934.*

Fallon, Tim P., S.J. and Riley, Philip Boo (Editors). Religion and Culture: Essays in Honor of Bernard Lonergan, S.J. New York: Suny, 1986.

Fessard, Gaston. De l'actualité historique. Paris: Desclée de Brouwer, 1960.*

Foucault, Michel. Language, Counter-Memory, Practice. Selected essays and interviews. Translated by Donald F. Bouchard and Sherry Simon. Ithaca, New York: Cornell University Press, 1977.

______. The Order of Things: An Archeology of Human Sciences. New York: Vintage Books, 1970. [Vintage Books Edition, 1973.]

Frings, Manfred S. Max Scheler. Pittsburg, Pa.: Duquesne University Press, 1965.*

Habermas, Jürgen. Communication and the Evolution of Society. Boston: Beacon Press, 1979.

______. Theorie des kommunikativen Handelns. Band 1: Handlungsrationalitat und gesellschaftliche Rationalisierung. Band 2: Zur Kritik der funktionalistischen Vernunft. Frankfurt am Main: Suhrkamp Verlag, 1981.

______. The Theory of Communicative Action Vol. One Reason and the Rationalization of Society, transl. by Thomas McCarthy. Boston: Beacon Press, 1984.

______. Zur Rekonstruktion des Historischen Materialismus. Suhrkamp Verlag, 1976.

Hegel, G. W. F. Phänomenologie des Geistes. Vol. 3. Edited by Eva Moldenhauer and Karl Markus Michel. Frankfurt am Main: Suhrkamp Verlag, 1970.*

Held, David. Introduction to Critical Theory: Horkheimer to Habermas. Berkeley: University of California Press, 1980.

Husserl, Edmund. Ideas: General Introduction to Pure Phenomenology. Translated by W. R. Boyce Gibson. London: Collier-MacMillan, 1962.

Kant, Immanuel. Critique of Pure Reason. Translated by Norman Kempt Smith. New York: St. Martin's Press, Toronto: Macmillan, 1929.*

______. Logic. Translated by Robert Hartman and Wolfgang Schwartz. Indianapolis and New York: Bobbs-Merrill, 1974.

Kojève, Alexandre. Introduction to the Reading of Hegel: Lectures on the Phenomenology of Spirit. Translated by James H. Nichlos, Jr. Edited by Allan Bloom. Assembled by Raymond Queneau.

Ithaca and London: Cornell University Press, 1980.

Kurzweil, Edith. The Age of Structuralism: Lévi-Strauss to Foucault. New York: Columbia University Press, 1980.

Lamb, Matthew L. (Editor). Creativity and Method: Essays in Honor of Bernard Lonergan, S.J. Milwaukee, Wisconsin: Marquette University Press, 1981.

______. History, Method and Theology: A Dialectical Comparison of Wilhelm Dilthey's Critique of Historical Reason and Bernard Lonergan's Meta-Methodology. Missoula, Montana: Scholars Press, 1978.

Langer, Susanne. Feeling and Form: A Theory of Art. New York: Charles Scribner's Sons, 1953.*

Lawrence, Frederick. (Editor). The Beginning and the Beyond: Papers from the Gadamer and Voegelin Conferences. Supplementary Issue of Lonergan Workshop, Volume 4. Chico, California: Scholars Press, 1984.

______. (Editor). Lonergan Workshop. Vol. 6. Atlanta, GA: Scholars Press, 1986.

Marx, Karl. Selected Writings. Edited by David McLellan. Oxford: Oxford University Press, 1977.

McCarthy, Thomas. The Critical Theory of Jürgen Habermas. Cambridge: the MIT Press, 1982.

McShane, Philip. (Editor). Language, Truth and Meaning. Notre Dame, Indiana: University of Notre Dame Press, 1972.

Neumann, Erich. The Origins and History of Consciousness. Translated by R. F. Hull. Bollingen Serries: Vol. 42. (Illustrated). New York: Princeton University Press, 1970.

Niel, Henri. De la Médiation dans la Philosophie de Hegel. Paris: Aubier, 1945.*

Norberg-Schulz, Christian. Genius Loci: Towards a Phenomenology of Architecture. New York: Rizzoli International Publications, 1979.

Norris, Christopher. Deconstruction: Theory and Practice. London and New York: Methuen, 1982.

Ong, Walter J. Orality and Literacy: The Technologizing of the Word. London and New York: Methuen, 1982.

Piaget, Jean. Etudes d'épistemologie génétique. [Studies in Genetic Epistemology.] Edited by W. E. Beth, W. Mays and J. Piaget. Vols. I-III. Paris: Presses Universitaire de France, 1957.*

______. Structuralism. Translated by C. Maschler. New York: Harper & Row, 1976.*

Plato. The Collected Dialogues of Plato. Edited by Edith Hamilton and Huntington Cairns. Princeton, N. J.: Princeton University Press, 1961.

Ricoeur, Paul. Freud and Philosophy, trans. Denis Savage. New Haven: Yale University Press, 1980.

Rorty, Richard. Philosophy and the Mirror of Nature. Princeton, N. J.: Princeton University Press, 1979.

Sala, Giovanni B. Das Apriori in der menschlichen Erkenntnis: Eine Studie über Kants Kritik der reinen Vernunft und Lonergans Insight. Meisenheim am Glan: Hain, 1971.

Scheler, Max. Ressentiment. Edited, with an Introduction by Lewis A. Coser. Translated by William W. Holdheim. New York: Schocken Books, 1961.*

Silverman, Hugh J. and Ihde, Don (Editors). Hermeneutics and Deconstruction. New York: SUNY Press, 1985.

Skinner, Quentin (Editor). The Return of Grand Theory in the Human Sciences. Cambridge: Cambridge University Press, 1985.

Solzshenitsyn, Aleksandr I. A World Split Apart: Commencement Address Delivered at Harvard University June 8, 1978. New York: Harper & Row, 1978.

Tracy, David. The Achievement of Bernard Lonergan. New York: Herder & Herder, 1970.

______. Blessed Rage for Order: The New Pluralism in Theology. New York: The Seabury Press, A Crossroad Book, 1975.

Voegelin, Eric. The Order and History. Vols. I-V. Louisiana University Press, 1956.*

Whitehead, Alfred North. Science in the Modern World. Lowell Lectures 1925. New York: Free Press, 1967.*

Winter, Gibson. Elements for a Social Ethics. New York: MacMillan, 1966, 1968.*

Articles

Aichele, Jr., George. "Hegel and Deconstruction." Cross Currents. Vol. 34. No. 1 (Spring 1984): 118-121.

Barden, Garrett. "Insight and Mirrors." Method: Journal of Lonergan Studies. Vol. 4. No. 2 (Oct 1986): 85-104.

Briggs, Kenneth A. "B. J. F. Lonergan Dies in Canada: Jesuit Was a Leading Theologian." The New York Times. (Nov 29, 1984): 18.

"Distinguished Theologian Lonergan Dies." National Jesuit News. (Dec 1984): 17-18.

Dombrowski, Daniel A. "Rorty and Mirror Images in St. Thomas." Method: Journal of Lonergan Studies. Vol. 4. No. 2 (Oct 1986): 108-114.

"Funeral Mass of the Resurrection for Reverend Father Bernard Joseph Francis Lonergan, S.J." A liturgy booklet. Church of Our Lady of Lourdes, Toronto. (November 29, 1984).

Hável, Vaclav. "Politika a svědomí." ["Politics and Conscience."] Svědectví: Czechoslovak Quarterly Review XVIII, No. 72 (Paris: Tigrid, 1984): 621-35.

Lamb, Matthew. "Christianity within the Political Dialectics of Community and Empire." Method: Journal of Lonergan Studies. Vol. 1, No. 1 (March 1983): 1-30.

Lawrence, Fred. "Lonergan: a Tribute." Boston College Biweekly. (January 17, 1985): 8.

Marsh, James. Dialectical Phenomenology: From Suspension to Suspicion" in Man and World 17. Netherlands: Martinus Nijhoff Publishers. (1984): 121-141.

______. "Heidegger's Overcoming of Metaphysics: A Critique" Journal of the British Society for Phenomenology Vol. 16 No. 1 (January 1985): 55-69.

McCarthy, Tim. "Catholic Theologian Bernard Lonergan dies at age 79." National Catholic Reporter. (December 7, 1984): 1 and 25.

Meynell, Hugo. "Reply to Garrett Barden." Method: Journal of Lonergan Studies. Vol. 4. No. 27 (Oct 1986): 105-107.

______. "Reversing Rorty." Method: Journal of Lonergan Studies. Vol. 3. No. 1 (1985): 31-48.

Perego, A. "Una nuova opinione sull' unità psicologica di Cristo." Divinitas 2 (1958): 409-424.*

Riley, Philip Boo. "The Meaning of History: Leo Straus and Bernard Lonergan on 'The Crisis of Modernity.'" Logos: Philosophic Issues in Christian Perspective. Philosophic Studies from the University of Santa Clara. Vol. 4 (1983): 71-100.

Swain, Bernard F. "Lonergan's framework for the future." Commonweal. Vol. 112, No. 2 (January 1985): 46-50.

"Theologian's life and work enriches Catholic thought." National Catholic Reporter. (December 7, 1984): 25.

Dissertations

Alberg, Jeremiah Lawrence. "The Notion of Genuinennes in Bernard Lonergan's Insight." Unpublished Master's dissertation, Department of Philosophy, Saint Louis University, 1981.

Klein, Dennis Daly. "Dimensions of Culture in the Thought of Bernard Lonergan." Unpublished Doctoral dissertation, Department of Philosophy, Boston College, 1975.

INDEX OF NAMES

INDEX OF NAMES